STUDENT POLITICS OF IIT MADRAS

OF THE STUDENTS, BY THE CHIEF, FOR THE PEOPLE

THAKUR SUSHANT SINGH JASWAL

BlueRose ONE .com
Stories Matter
NewDelhi • London

BLUEROSE PUBLISHERS
India | U.K.

BlueRose ONE.com
Stories Matter
NewDelhi • London

For permissions requests or inquiries regarding this publication, please contact:

BLUEROSE PUBLISHERS
www.BlueRoseONE.com
info@bluerosepublishers.com
+91 8882 898 898
+4407342408967

ISBN: 978-93-6783-013-0

Cover design: Shubham
Typesetting: Sagar

First Edition: January 2025

"Kāk cheṣṭā, bako dhyānam, śvān nidrā tathaiva cha,
alpāhārī, gṛhatyāgī, vidyārthī ke pañch lakṣaṇ."

Om Gan Ganpatāye Namāha!

Acknowledgment

I would like to express my heartfelt gratitude to the following individuals for their invaluable contributions to the successful completion of this book:

My sincere thanks to my parents, Ms. Rita Devi and Mr. Rajneesh Jaswal, who have been guiding lights throughout my life and have played an indispensable role in the realisation of this book. I am also deeply grateful to my younger sister, Ms. Hashi Jaswal, who set high benchmarks by successfully publishing two books herself and guiding a novice like me in the field of writing.

I extend my heartfelt appreciation to my paternal grandparents, Shri Om Prakash Jaswal and Smt. Pushpa Devi (village Amlehar, HP), my maternal grandparents, Honorary Captain Mehar Singh Rana (Retd.), and Smt. Sheela Devi (village Raipur, HP). A special mention goes to my paternal uncle and aunt, Mr. Daljeet Jaswal and Ms. Neelam Jaswal, for their care and support during my time in Himachal.

This book would have remained just an idea if not for the constant motivation from my HS20 Boys' gang: Prem M., Vishal Singh, Appukrishnan M.V., Botta Demudu Naidu, Vaibhav Awasthi, Lara Thomas, Anand R., Shubham Uikey, Abhishek Barua, Abhiram V.M., and Yatin Satish. They are more than just classmates; they are brothers who stood by me during challenging times, always putting my needs before their own.

My experiences with SECC would have been incomplete without the mentorship and guidance of my seniors—Mihir Chawla, Saket Saurabh, and Ardra S. Shibu—whom I continue to turn to for advice and support. I must also acknowledge the crucial roles played by Kaushik Raja, Trivikram Satharasi, Karthik Kurimindla, Naincy Sachan, Karishma K.S., Akhil Koshy, Ishwarya Ganesh, Mohammad Zaid, and Tejaswini Jagtap, who made my SECC journey unforgettable.

Among the professors, I am profoundly grateful to Prof. Anup Kumar Bhandari for his thoughtful guidance during moments of uncertainty. Special thanks to Prof. Anbarasu M., Prof. Sudakar Chandran, Prof. Jeganmohan Reddy, and Prof. V. Sriram for their unwavering support to SEC as the Election Officers. I also feel privileged to have the friendship of Prof. Sathyanarayana N. Gummadi, who, as the Dean of Students at IIT Madras, is not only an excellent administrator but also a genuinely kind-hearted individual.

I am particularly thankful to Dr. Jinna Bordoloi, an exceptional clinical psychologist and a remarkable individual whose critical insights helped me incorporate significant suggestions.

My heartfelt gratitude goes to Mr. Sanidhya Chaturvedi, who not only took time out of his busy schedule to write the foreword for my book but also reviewed it critically. He is one of the most inspiring seniors I have met at IIT Madras—witty, approachable, and genuinely supportive.

I am also grateful to Ms. Robin Rathi (RAS 2024-25), Ms. Meenakshi Anoop (SECC & SEC Chief Commissioner 2024-25), and Mr. Aaromal S. Kesav (Cultural Affairs Secretary, Arts 2024-25) for their kindness and support. Many thanks to Mr. Neetesh Meena for providing valuable insights into IITM student politics.

Lastly, I honor the IITM student politics and everyone associated with it in any capacity. Many individuals have made this journey memorable, whether by collaborating with me or by choosing to oppose me. I respect the presence of each person I encountered during my college life, as they provided me with valuable experiences, both good and bad. I firmly believe in the saying, "Good times test you, and bad times teach you." I not only discovered the true meaning of this through my active participation in IITM student politics but also through my commitment to regulating it on ethical grounds.

Preface

Thakur Sushant Singh Jaswal is a final-year student at the Indian Institute of Technology, Madras, pursuing an Integrated MA in Development Studies. He is passionate about exploring new tasks and taking on challenges to enhance his skill set and accomplishments. Since his school days, he has been actively involved in student politics, serving as Head Boy (Class V), Vice President (Class XI), and President (Class XII) at Ryan International School, Noida. Originally from the small village of Amlehar in Himachal Pradesh, he is now a permanent resident of Delhi NCR.

In terms of accolades, he is a Bharat Scouts & Guides Governor's Awardee (2016) and holds an NCC 'C' Certificate with an 'A' grade (2023) as the Cadet Senior Under Officer of the 4 (TN) Air Sqn (Tech) NCC at IIT Madras. In 2023, he was also honored with the Institute Merit Award for his exceptional academic performance in his department. Sushant has significant experience in academic writing and research within the social sciences. He has interned as a research analyst at the Reserve Bank of India, Chennai (2023), as a research assistant at IIT Delhi (2022), as a research analyst at the Centre for Air Power Studies (2022), and as a content writer for MyGov under the Prime Minister's Office (2021).

Sushant is the former Chief Commissioner of the Student Ethics and Constitution Commission (SECC) and the Student Election Commission (SEC) of IIT Madras, where he played a pivotal role in conducting India's first blockchain-based campus elections in 2023. Having been a part of SECC and SEC for the past three years, this book is the culmination of his experiences and contributions during that time.

Over his five years at IIT Madras, Sushant has gained first-hand experience in navigating the post-pandemic normalcy of campus life. From serving as a Head to becoming a Chief in the student government bodies (SECC and SEC), he has not only immersed himself in the student politics of IIT Madras but has also made a lasting impact for future generations to remember.

In 2024, Sushant undertook the serious endeavor of writing this book following the successful publication of his earlier work, *The Jaswan Chronicles: Rediscovering One of the Oldest Himachal Pradesh Clans*, earlier that year. Despite balancing academic pressures, leading one of IITM's most bureaucratic student bodies, engaging with diverse individuals, and meticulously analyzing official records and cases, Sushant successfully compiled three transformative years of his life into this book. This work is not just a reflection on his past but also a constructive critique of the present state of IITM student politics, aimed at fostering a brighter future for the upcoming generations of IIT Madras students.

Foreword

It is with immense pride and enthusiasm that I write this foreword for a work that goes beyond the realm of mere pages–it embodies the spirit of conviction, reform, and student-driven governance. This book, penned by my junior and a fellow visionary leader, Sushant Singh Jaswal, captures the intricate journey of student politics at IIT Madras. His role as the Chief Commissioner of the Student Ethics and Constitution Commission (SECC) and a pivotal figure in conducting India's first blockchain-based campus election as the Chief Election Commissioner of Student Election Commission (SEC) reflects the depth of his dedication and the pioneering impact of his contributions.

In the corridors of IIT Madras, where brilliance meets relentless ambition, Sushant's experiences represent a rare confluence of ethical leadership, bureaucratic acumen, and unshakable resolve. His narrative delves into the unseen dynamics of student governance–the alliances, challenges, and ethical dilemmas that shape the democratic foundations of our student body. The book is more than a recounting of events; it is a bold critique and a blueprint for future leaders to craft a more transparent and inclusive governance structure.

What makes this work truly stand apart is the sincerity with which it confronts systemic issues while holding steadfast to a vision of protopia—a society where progress is perpetual. It reveals how the interplay of identity, meritocracy, and politics can influence governance in unexpected ways. Sushant's honest reflections, combined with a deep respect for constitutional integrity, invite every reader to think critically about the power of student leadership and the enduring lessons it holds for life beyond the gates of academia.

To my fellow students, future leaders, and readers who believe in the transformative power of politics—this book will stir your curiosity, challenge your perspectives, and ignite your passion for responsible governance. It is not just a testimony to the spirit of IIT Madras but a timeless reminder that even in the microcosm of student life, the seeds of national and global leadership are sown.

I commend Sushant for his courage, dedication, and pursuit of truth. May his words inspire you as they have inspired me.

– Sanidhya Chaturvedi
Co-Founder, Director and CEO, Folium Sensing Pvt Ltd
Student at Dept of Electrical Engineering, IITM

Contents

Chapter 1

Student Government Structure of IIT Madras

After a long haul of consistent academic confrontations and accomplishments, every Indian kid aspires to be a student at IIT - the Indian Institute of Technology. These IITs are not just prominent higher educational institutes of India but are a gateway to a promising future that every kid dreams to realise for a better life. The symbolic meaning that the IITs hold today's date is an accumulation of people's perceptions along with the significant scientific contributions that these institutions have made for the greater good of humanity. With India aiming to become the knowledge economy of the world, India currently consists of 23 - IITs, 31 - NITs (National Institute of Technology) and 26 - IIITs (Indian Institutes of Information Technology). For the emerging middle class these educational institutes especially IITs are a medium through which they earn cultural and social capital which can later be converted to economic capital to improve their standards of living.

To realise my IITian dream I along with thousands of other students from different socio-cultural backgrounds finally made it to the No. 1 higher educational institute of India i.e. IIT Madras in the year 2020. IIT Madras offers multiple unique programs in a variety of disciplines ranging from Computer Science to English Studies. While majority of the students had cleared JEE Mains & JEE Advance to take admission at IIT Madras to pursue B.Tech. In juxtaposition, I took admission at IIT Madras through an unconventional approach which was coincidental to a significant extent. I was a student who had pursued humanities with maths in class 12th and was looking forward to being admitted to a college that provided me with a bachelor's degree in economics. Being a humanities student, my board exams' aggregate percentage was enough to secure me a seat at one of the renowned Delhi University Colleges. But the little ambitious me wanted to take an entrance exam to get admitted to any one of the reputed colleges. One week after my birthday I was randomly surfing through the internet for the entrance exams that the students of humanities can take after completing their intermediate. I came across an exam that not only fulfilled my wish of clearing an entrance exam but also allowed me to fulfill my father's dream of becoming an IITian. At the last hour of the last day to fill out the application form, I registered for the exam which neither I nor my known had ever heard of it.

At the age of 18, in my first attempt, I secured an All India Rank - 15 in the Humanities and Social Sciences Entrance Exam - 2020 (HSEE - 2020). The exam was conducted annually by IIT Madras, specifically by the Humanities and Social Sciences Department (HSS) for students who are interested in pursuing their career either in Development Studies or English Studies for 5 years. The Integrated MA Degree in Development Studies (branch of Development Economics) was one of the most unique degrees in India which is offered by a handful of institutes like IIT Madras and Tata Institute of Social Sciences (TISS). However, the program and the exam were discontinued in the year 2023. With the advent of the COVID-19 pandemic, HSEE was postponed twice and the result was declared in October 2020. I got enrolled in the program in November and my classes started from the 3rd week of the same month in an online format.

Challenging times seek challenging solutions, I had a virtual orientation session where I was informed about the institute and the campus life in the most mundane manner. There was no immersion program for us like it used to be conducted, nor was there any orientation session conducted by any student secretary. All I knew was that I had taken admission at IIT Madras where only professors guide us through our academic pursuits and nothing else. For the next 6 months, I had completed 3 trimesters which was equivalent to completing 2 semesters and I had no idea about the campus life because I didn't know anyone from IIT Madras.

Knowing about campus life itself was so difficult for me, getting to know about the student politics at IIT Madras was a shot in the dark. But this is not the case for you all, so let me introduce you all to the student political structure of IIT Madras in a formal manner. And give you all a headstart in this rollercoaster journey of mine where my actions were louder than my words.

Politics is the backbone of any desirable social structure that one envisages for a quasi-community to follow and evolve into a society that achieves the greater purpose of having such a society. The purpose behind the formation of IIT Madras was to produce learned tech graduates who will act as responsible future citizens of India and will contribute to India's growth endeavors in all possible manners. Keeping the same idea in mind, the drafters of the Students' Constitution of IIT Madras came up with a unique political structure that allowed students to enjoy the essence of democracy with enough freedom given to them to experiment with versatile political ideas. The current Students' Constitution of IIT Madras came into force in 2017 and officially gives legal backing to all the students' activities within the precincts of IIT Madras.[1]

The 49-page document contains a Preamble, 11 Chapters, 29 Sections, and 150 Clauses that are enough to regulate, facilitate, and coordinate the ever-expanding student population of IIT Madras (IITM). Surprisingly, the document that has been shaping the campus life of every student is least known to the students at IITM. Or to put it in another manner, the Constitution *(Chapter I, Clause III)* that considers the students (General Student Body - GSB) the supreme power in the governmental setup are unaware of any such power and often become subordinate to such governmental setup. Is it intentional or unintentional? We will come to know by the end of this book. The Students' Constitution enshrines 9 Fundamental Rights (Rights of Students) and 9 Fundamental Duties (Responsibilities of Students) which most of the students are unaware of until their graduation. This is because, to date, there has been no detailed or focused orientation on this subject matter by any student government official or by any professor during the immersion programs for freshers. Any attempt to spread awareness about the same at the later stage of the college often invites apathy and indifference, which is natural considering the hectic timetable of an average IITM student.

The Student Government structure as mentioned in the Students' Constitution consists of three branches which have been explicitly mentioned in Fig 1. The three branches of democracy - legislature, executive, and judiciary are embodied by the Student Legislative Council (SLC), Executive Council (EC), and Student Ethics & Constitution Commission (SECC) respectively at IIT Madras. Like any other form of democracy, the three branches of democracy at IITM also kept a checks and balances system in place. The SLC is enshrined with the legislative powers to legislate bills, resolutions, and constitutional amendments. The EC is responsible for the seamless execution of the passed legislation and their respective constitutional responsibilities. The SECC is responsible for regulating the GSB by acting as a custodian, interpreter and preacher of the Students' Constitution of IIT Madras. All the members of the government are addressed as Student Government Officials who are expected to maintain the highest level of ethical standards during the term of their office. SECC is one of the peculiar branches of student government as it is a quasi-judicial and completely bureaucratic student body of IIT Madras. SECC comprises a Chief Commissioner who is the *ex-officio* head of the organisation and 2 Commissioners who have equal powers and responsibilities to that of the Chief. On the other hand, there are 59 legislators in SLC along with a Speaker who is part of the executive council that comprises 10 members. All these positions are often termed PoR (Position of Responsibility) which is more common to hear in insti lingo (words that are colloquially used in IIT Madras) than to come across them in any formal document.

The term PoR is defined as any student or student body who possesses executive or decision-making power within that organisation. The different types of student bodies or organisations that act as the foundation of the PoR culture can be divided into 3 broad types.

1. **Student Government Associated Organisations (SGAO)** - that are under the purview of either EC/SLC/SECC and can use Gymkhana Funds. Eg. EML (Extra Mural Lectures)[1*]
2. **Board of Student Associated Organisations/ Independent Student Bodies (ISB)** - are independent of the student government and cannot use Gymkhana Funds. Eg. Vande Matram[2*]
3. **Institute Organisations** - student organisations that report directly either to the Director or Deans. Eg. MITR[3*]

[1*] EML is the official Lec-Dem body of IITM established in 1982. YouTube - youtube.com/c/emliitm

[2*] Vande Matram founded in 2015, aims to sensitize students about India's rich cultural, economic, social, scientific, economic and technological heritage. YouTube - https://www.youtube.com/@VandeMataramIITMadras

[3*] MITR founded in 2018, is the student wellness body of IIT Madras that comes under the direct purview of Dean of Students.

While going through the different types of student bodies you all must be thinking about what Gymkhana Funds refer to - well, it is the corpus of funds that is the aggregate of the students' fees.

The moment freshers meet their seniors, the most common topic of discussion is regarding PoR and its related merits and demerits. PoRs provide a forum through which students interact with students from other departments and programs to collectively achieve unified goals. These same PoRs often become the grounds of political trade and the stepping stones for better placements or internships in reputed firms.

Fig. 1 - Student Government Structure of IIT Madras[4*]

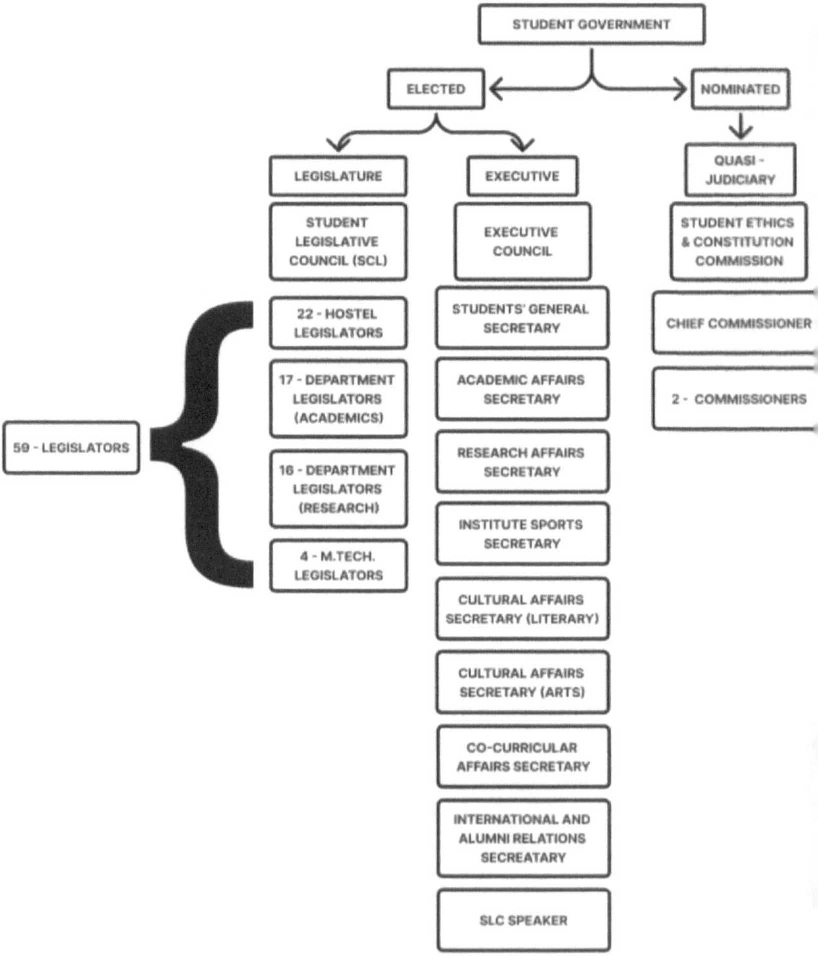

[4*] The table has been created by the author based on the past election notifications published by the DoST Office of IIT Madras until 2024, and is subject to change.

But the 18-year-old me sitting in one corner of the room in front of a 13-inch MacBook was still trying to figure out the suitable PoR for himself. Unaware of either the PoR culture or the important student bodies, I randomly applied for 7 PoRs out of which I was able to secure 6 PoRs in different capacities in different teams ranging from EML, Sports Organisation Committee (SOC) to Global Engagement Events' Team. Among all these PoRs, the only PoR that excited me the most was the position of Constitutional Monitoring and Operations Head (CMOH) which is part of the Head of Secretariat of SECC. This is because I aspire to become a civil servant and the only PoR that gave me the feel of working in a bureaucratic organisation as a fresher was the position of CMOH.

At the time of writing the lengthy application for CMOH, I had read the Students' Constitution multiple times but was unable to comprehend it because of a lack of practical knowledge which was evident to the Commissioners at the time of my interview. On receiving the affirmative response regarding my selection as the CMOH at SECC, I was at the peak of my happiness as I felt this is one of the best PoRs that a fresher could get because of the power with which it comes along.

From that day onwards, I believe my campus life actually began because I was following my passion and was not part of the rat race to seek a PoR with high-paying job prospects. Most people know that IITs provide high-paying job offers but they don't know that to achieve one such offer one either needs to have a high CGPA/ a PoR peak/ International exposure along with a desirable skill set. The recruiters of the companies who are the alumni of IITM are well aware of the PoR culture and often recruit those students who have experience in those PoRs that have a long history of existence in IITM. Being unaware and carefree of all these intricacies I was blindly following my passion because any experience that brings me closer to my ultimate goal of becoming a civil servant was the experience that I was always looking forward to.

Never did I realise that I was working in a team that is not just rare to see in any college across India but is also rare to find in any other IITs. Being the only student bureaucratic organisation at IIT Madras, SECC allowed me to experience student politics from a very different perspective because SECC is the same organisation that acts as the Student Election Commission (SEC) at the time of student elections. In short, I was in a team of *babus* (a term used for civil servants in India) who were students by nature but were bureaucrats by profession which is nothing less than having a square peg in a round hole. The reason why I say this is because both the roles of a student and a bureaucrat are contrary to each other. The former is in the stage of exploring life while the latter is in the stage of shaping the lives of others. This can be one of the reasons why most of the IITs don't have any student bureaucratic body similar to SECC (refer to Table 1).

IIT Name	Student Govt.	Constitution	Student Quasi-Judicial Body
Indian Institute of Technology (IIT), Gandhi Nagar	YES	YES	NO
Indian Institute of Technology (IIT), Bhubaneshwar	YES	YES	NO
Indian Institute of Technology (IIT), Madras	YES	YES	YES
Indian Institute of Technology (IIT), Guwahati	YES	YES	NO
Indian Institute of Technology (IIT), Indore	YES	YES	NO
Indian Institute of Technology (IIT), Kanpur	YES	YES	NO
Indian Institute of Technology (IIT), Jodhpur	YES	YES	NO

Indian Institute of Technology (IIT), Kharagpur	YES	YES	NO
Indian Institute of Technology (IIT), Hyderabad	YES	YES	NO
Indian Institute of Technology (IIT), Mumbai	YES	YES	NO
Indian Institute of Technology (IIT), Patna	YES	YES	NO
Indian Institute of Technology (IIT), Delhi	YES	YES	NO
Indian Institute of Technology (IIT), Ropar	YES	YES	NO
Indian Institute of Technology (IIT), Mandi	YES	YES	NO
Indian Institute of Technology (IIT), Roorkee	YES	YES	NO

Indian Institute of Technology (Banaras Hindu University), Varanasi	YES	YES	NO
Indian Institute of Technology (IIT), Jammu	YES	YES	NO
Indian Institute of Technology (IIT), Palakkad	YES	YES	NO
Indian Institute of Technology (IIT), Tirupati	YES	YES	NO
Indian Institute of Technology (IIT), Goa	YES	YES	NO
Indian Institute of Technology (IIT), Bhilai	YES	YES	NO
Indian Institute of Technology (IIT) Dharwad	YES	YES	NO

Indian Institute of Technology (Indian School of Mines), Dhanbad	YES	YES	NO

Table 1 - Data showing the presence of Student Govt., Students' Constitution & Student Quasi-Judicial body across IITs[5*]

As a counter-argument, I believe that the purpose of having a student bureaucratic body is to holistically have a student government structure where the faculty has the sole role of guidance and facilitation. In other IITs faculty is also treated to be the functioning members of the student government structure often leading to the liberty of such governments getting compromised. This is because all these IITs don't have anyone to play the role of opposition other than the faculty that regulates or constructively criticises the actions of the student government officials for the greater good of the students. However, SECC plays the role of opposition too where it constructively criticises the actions of the GSB as well as the student government officials by justifying the constitutional validity of their actions and accordingly regulating them. Hence, in my opinion, the student government structure of IITM is one of the most student-centric and democratic forms of student government where all the checks and balances are conducted by the students, for the students, and of the students.

[5*] The data has been solely collected and organised by the author as per the information available till November 2024 and is subject to change.

Although there is an oxymoronic relationship that seems to exist in the term student bureaucratic organisation it allowed students like me who wish to experience bureaucracy during their student life and subsequently shape their demeanor for a desirable future. However, this oxymoronic relationship takes a heavy toll on the members of the SECC because of the peculiar role that the SECC has to play. As per the *Rules of Procedure* of SECC, the purpose of the organisation is '*To serve the students of IIT Madras by exercising powers of judicial review, regulation, accountability and corrective measures to aid the cause of a more harmonious union of students at IIT Madras, guided by the principles of liberty, equality and justice under the constitution.*'[2]

In the process of fulfilling its duties, SECC often is treated as the 'other' by the GSB, the one who acts with more maturity and accountability than any student body at IITM. Because of such a treatment, the members of the SECC especially the commissioners have to negotiate with their personal lives multiple times for the sake of the organisation's integrity and students' faith that they all enshrine in SECC if GSB faces any injustice during their college life. Like in any other trial, there would always be a party that would win a case against the other. Similar is the scenario with SECC where a party would win over the other, often leading to praises from the former and criticisms from the latter to SECC. However, SECC's objective is to deliver justice to both parties irrespective of the case because both parties are comprised of students who are still in the process of becoming mature. But does that mean are the members of SECC mature enough to deliver justice to the parties who are of alike age? Or does that mean SECC comprises students who have some special attributes that other students don't have? Well, I leave the answers to these questions to you all because I firmly believe that you will arrive at your respective answers by the end of this book without fail.

I as a former member of SECC am going to unveil the IITM student politics with utmost sincerity and candor to constructively analyse and criticise the existing student government at IITM for the greater good of everyone. The greater objective of this book is to uncover the political facet of campus life for the people outside IIT to know about the advancements that India's No. 1 educational institute has made when it comes to student politics. The following book delves into the student politics of IITM in an autobiographical manner, where I will be revealing about the student politics following my 3 years of experience at SECC. All the mentioned information in this book is my personal opinions collated with the published information that has been posted by SECC on its official website. In no manner, I attempt to fabricate any false information or communicate any false claim regarding IIT Madras or any associated student organisation through my book. Keeping the integrity of my past positions at SECC, I would be ensuring the confidentiality of all types of sensitive information as my utmost priority.

Chapter 2

The Sleeper Build - CMOH (2021-2022)

The motto of SECC is *'Bonum Commune Communitatis'* which stands for the common good of the society. At first glance, the philosophical root of this motto seems to be utilitarianism which seeks the greater good for a greater number of people. With this school of thought one can easily interpret the imminent message of this motto that the individual's good can be compromised for the greater good of the community which is true to a certain extent. However, the practical meaning of this motto can be understood through a different philosophical school which is egoistic altruism, which stands for the actions that seem to be altruistic but are motivated by self-interest. This way there seems to be a negotiation and re-negotiation between the individual rights and the community good that is more common to see in the student politics than the utilitarian approach.

The same was the case with me too as I had applied for the position of CMOH to satisfy my ego and perform all the duties that mutually benefited both the GSB and my PoR.

The position of Constitutional Monitoring & Operations Head is responsible for ensuring the appropriate implementation of the Students' Constitution by acting as a whistleblower for SECC and confirming the constitutional validity of any student action at IIT Madras at a rudimentary level. Being the first CMOH of the institute had put more responsibilities over my shoulders than any other PoR. This is because I had to prove the purpose of the position not just to the GSB but even to SECC. So was the case of my fellow Head of Secretariats - Events Head (Ms. Ishwarya Ganesh) and Design Head (Mr. Mohammad Zaid) who were amazing people to come across in my campus life.

Among the three of us, the Events Head was the only one who had experienced the Students' General Elections (SGE) earlier during that year (2021) as part of the SEC. Me and the Design Head being new to this sphere were still trying to get the hang of the political scenario of IITM. Based on our limited anticipation of the insti political scenario, we all brainstormed together when everyone was confronting the pandemic to conduct new outreach and publicity events for SECC and SEC. Finally, we came up with the unique idea of starting a flagship lecture series that invites people from different dimensions of the political system of India ranging from bureaucracy to academia to encourage and enlighten the political acumen among the students.

Our first speaker was the then-acting Chief Election Commissioner of India Mr. Sushil Chandra who was generous enough to accept our invitation to be the first speaker of Voices of the State. We arranged a YouTube live session with Mr. Chandra and it was an honor for me to host the session. Many students and faculty attended the session as it was themed around the topic of Elections in India. In the post-session analysis, we understood that our flagship lecture series proved helpful for students as we were appreciated by many for conducting such an informative session. As a matter of fact, it was astonishing for Mr. Chandra to realise that there is another (Student) Chief Election Commissioner other than him who had invited him for a lecture.

The lecture given by Mr. Chandra revolved around the importance of elections in a democracy and the procedure of conducting General Elections in India.[3] If we compare it with our campus elections, it is quite different. In the Students' General Elections (SGE) of IITM, we have a preferential voting mechanism where each voter has to give preferences for each candidate who is contesting for a particular position. In addition to this, each voter is given the option of abstain (the voter chooses to not cast her vote for that particular post) as well as rejection (the voter chooses to reject all the contesting candidates for the post; similar to None of The Above [NOTHA]). Each IITM voter has three options to select from either she has to give preferences or choose to abstain or choose rejection.

IITM has been conducting online elections since 2017 and has stopped using the ballot paper voting system to make progress in electoral technology. The counting of the votes in SGE starts only if these two conditions are fulfilled - (i) More than 50% of the electorate has cast non-abstain votes for the post (ii) Of the total non-abstain votes polled, more than 50% have not rejected all the candidates.[4] Subsequently, two types of vote-counting methods are used after the above two conditions are met, the appropriate method is being used depending on the number of contesting candidates. The two methods are First Past the Posts and Instant Runoff Voting Posts. The former refers to the situation when there are at least two candidates and if one of them receives more than 50% of non-abstained votes then that candidate shall be declared the winner. The latter refers to a situation where more than two candidates are contesting for a position and if none of them receives more than 50% of non-abstained votes then, the candidate with the least preference shall be eliminated. Her vote share shall be divided among other candidates as per their subsequent preferences. This process shall keep on going until a candidate receives more than 50% of non-abstained votes.

To deal with such a sophisticated type of election, the voters need to be sophisticated enough to critically compare the candidates and make a meaningful decision. This is because the majority of the time, winners are never decided by the 1st preference but are always decided by the 2nd, 3rd, and subsequent preferences. We all usually take it for granted that IITians are the smartest people on earth; hence, they always use their brains before performing any action. Unsurprisingly, this is not the case because IITians are humans too, and not just manufactured machines out of a factory. Most of the students at IITM are not even aware that elections are taking place in the institute. Over and above it, getting to know the candidates who are contesting for a particular position is too cumbersome a process. First of all, most of the IITMians are short on time as a resource to be invested in Students' General Elections (SGE) where they have to know the candidates first and then make an informed decision. On average, every hosteler IITMian has to vote for 9 executive council members + 7 hostel council members + 1 department legislator = 17 posts. If we assume that for every post there are at least two candidates who are contesting for the position then that means, an IITMian voter has to take into account 34 candidates at the time of casting a vote.

Secondly, the IITMian voters have to engage with the candidates and know about their manifesto only within (approx.) 14 working days which is the same time when either Quiz 1 or Quiz 2 happens. In such a tight schedule, expecting the voters to cast votes sincerely is few and far between. This creates a precarious situation for the voters to rely solely on word of mouth rather than reason and logic to exercise their freedom of expression. On the other hand, candidates are well aware of this situation and often create strategies to reap benefits from this political apathy among the voters.

As per the Election Manual, all candidates shall be contesting independently and hence there will be no party politics as is usually seen in a democracy. In reality, the close friends of the candidates generally function like a party that campaigns on her behalf and helps the candidates throughout the elections. For ease of reading, I shall be addressing the friends of these candidates as 'candidate preachers' who have a vital role in the candidate's campaigning. The candidate preachers support the candidate because they are close friends and would support each other irrespective of any situation. These candidate preachers then create 'candidate mongers' who would support the candidate only because their seniors or friends have asked them to do so even though they don't have a direct relationship with the candidate. The candidate preachers and mongers are of varying ages and diverse departments.

The only difference between these two categories of students is that the preachers are directly while the mongers are indirectly related to the candidate. Depending on their program and academic year, at the time of elections, they devote their time to support the candidate. As the academic year passes, academic engagement becomes comparatively less demanding, and the students spend more time in elections than they could have done in their first or second year. Similarly, B.Tech students from all the departments during the elections are more active than the PhD, MA, M.Tech, or M.Sc students. This simple logic can be understood through the given figure as well.

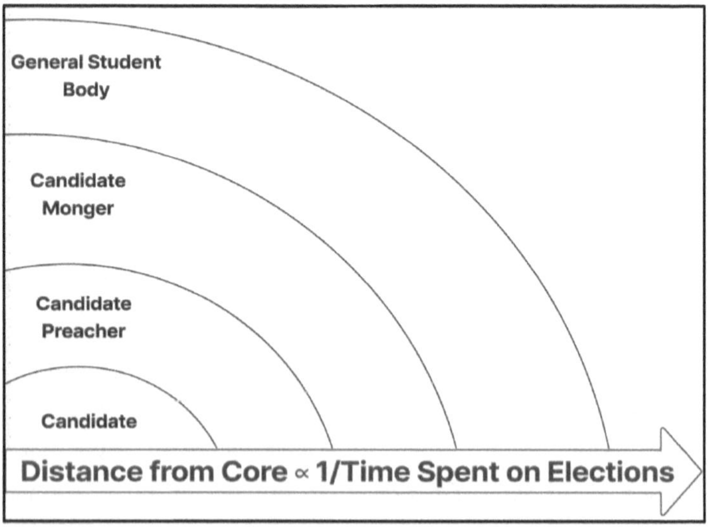

Fig. 2 - Time spent by the Candidate (Core) and the GSB (Periphery) on Elections

The figure explains that the students who spend more time on the student elections are usually the students in their pre-final or final year. With so many commitments in hand, taking the responsibility to contest elections and eventually win them, candidates are often tempted to take the help of a set of students who are well aware of each nook and corner of the elections. These students have witnessed the SGEs for at least 4 years and have a firm hold on their vote bank. Yes! You read it correctly. A vote bank consisting of students, segregated into decisive linguistic and regional groups becomes active during campus elections.

Such students are called 'Gawds' who are well aware of the demand & supply of SGE and are experts in creating strategies for the candidates to win at any cost. By the term demand and supply, I am referring to the demand of votes from the desperate candidates to win the elections and the supply of votes from the indifferent GSB who cast their vote only if there is any meaningful return. These Gawds come into action when freshers enter the institute by highlighting the commonalities between them like language and region. These Gawds are undoubtedly very helpful but cunning enough to expect a favor in return. The favor is to support the Gawds and depend on Gawds for anything and everything in the institute. Hence, the informal hierarchy among the GSB that becomes active at the time of SGE is mentioned here in the descending order of power - Gawd, Candidate, Candidate Preacher, Candidate Monger, and GSB which is collectively addressed as backend. Among them 'Gawds' are the only ones who are very difficult to identify because of their inconspicuous identity.

At the time of SGE, the candidates reach out to these Gawds for fundaes but often end up being part of discriminative deals that exploit the precarious situations of candidates and the voters. The deals here refer to the negotiations these Gawds make among themselves to distribute the executive council positions among the selected regional and linguistic groups. Accordingly, the vote bank of each segmented group is convinced to vote for that particular candidate who is contesting for the position that is in alignment with her identity. For instance, the Students' General Secretary position is always contested by students from North Indian states who are usually Hindi speakers. On the other hand, position like Hostel Affairs Secretary is always dominated by Telugu-speaking students. Simultaneously, positions like Academic Affairs Secretary are contested between two or more identity groups, leading to friction among these groups. As per the insti lingo, there are broadly 4 identity groups created based on language and region - Northies, Gults, Malus, and Tams. Northies refer to all the students who hail from the Hindi-speaking belt and belong to the states north of Karnataka and Andhra Pradesh. Gults refer to the Telugu-speaking students, Malus refer to the Malayalam-speaking students and Tams refer to the Tamil-speaking students.

These identity groups foster destructive unity which is highly harmful to the GSB and the fruitful functioning of the student government body of IIT Madras in the long run. Although at the individual and short-term level, such unity may be rewarding. But sprouting the sense of identity politics among the students at the time of elections is the death of the democratic spirit of student politics where identity is preferred over meritocracy. One can notice that the fate of the student government body is decided by a handful of students rather than the GSB which is supposed to be the supreme power in IITM as per its Students' Constitution.

This situation is the result of multi-faceted factors ranging from the student government officials to the GSB that function in an interconnected fashion for their selfish gains. The root cause of this whole issue is the lack of free and formal communication about student politics at IITM. The day freshers are inducted in IITM there is no separate orientation to sensitize the students about the evils of the student politics that can hamper their peaceful living in the institute. Till today, freshers get to know about student politics through informal talks with their seniors and often end up holding on to false impressions about the SGEs. False impressions like one needs to take help from the Gawds to win the elections even for the post of Hostel Legislator. Therefore, the elections that were supposed to happen independent of any party politics end up having identity politics which is more dangerous than anything else. The identity politics becomes so dominant that the students start holding on to the prejudices against each other which kills the idea of having a demographically diverse campus. Having a numerically diverse campus and having a culturally diverse campus are two different things. All IITs aim to have a culturally diverse campus to promote the idea of universal citizenship where students work selflessly for the greater good of humanity. Unfortunately, IITs are still struggling to achieve such a utopian situation because no one is putting genuine effort into correcting these social evils.

However, the pandemic acted like a structural break which jolted this whole system to a significant extent. The freshers of the 2021 batch were no longer interested in the petty business of elections because they were unable to make sense of it as they had never lived IITM's campus life. Then came the time of the year when Students' General Elections 2022 was conducted and only a handful of students were allowed to stay on campus along with the 2020 batch. All other batches were asked to join the campus later because of the quarantine measures that the institute had to take to control the spread of the pandemic. Being the CMOH of the institute, I assisted the SECC Commissioners in all their tasks for the fruitful conduct of SGE 2022. This was the time when I closely observed the backstage efforts that went into conducting the month-long elections where administration, students, and faculty worked hand-in-hand to complete the event successfully. My close counter with all these identity groups happened when we organised the Soapboxes for the post of executive council members in SGE 2022.

Soapboxes refer to an open platform where all the candidates sit together for an open debate officially conducted by the SEC. SEC decided to stream it live on its YouTube channel because the pandemic guidelines were stringent enough to constrain the number of soapbox attendees. One of the soapboxes where one could easily see the identity groups active in its extreme form was the position of Cultural Affairs Secretary (Literary). Only two candidates were contesting for this particular post but both were from different regional and linguistic backgrounds. The soapbox was conducted in CLT (Central Lecture Theatre) and only 150 students were allowed to sit inside the hall at a designated time. Around 60% of the CLT was filled by one identity group and the rest of the 40% by the other group. Seeing the dominant voice of one group, students of the latter group started crowding in front of the CLT to get inside the hall to show their dominance.

Standing in front of the CLT gate and controlling the frenzied crowd was nothing less than a nightmare. I still remember the arguments that the candidate preachers and mongers were making to enter the hall. Few of them were saying that it is their political right to support their candidates and attend the soapbox. While others were like at least allow the females to enter the hall since they would get tired by standing outside the CLT. Even though not a single seat was vacant in the CLT, the frenzied crowd got inside the CLT by pushing us aside and sat down over the stairs to support their candidate.

During the time of soapbox, whenever a candidate would answer a question in a taunting manner, the supporters of the candidate would yell at the top of their voices. While the opposing group would constantly do the booing to reciprocate their dominance. Not even a single student among the audience attends the soapbox for the sake of attending the soapbox. Students attend the soapbox either to support their candidate irrespective of the answers that she is giving, or they attend the soapbox to get entertainment which they eagerly look forward to. On the contrary, soapboxes are meant to intriguingly question the manifesto and feasibility report of the candidate, based on which the candidate gives her response.

During the soapbox of the Cultural Affairs Secretary (Literary), one of the students (Gawd) asked a question regarding the validity of the malpractices that the opposing candidate's supporters had been doing to demean the other candidate. In response to this, someone from the audience passed a taunting comment which led to a verbal scuffle among the two groups. The scuffle became so violent that the soapbox had to be terminated at that moment, and the IITM police had to be called to control the crowd. With the completion of the soapboxes, we had the D-day of SGE 2022 i.e. the polling day, the day when the majority of the students cast their votes from the comfort of their houses.

However, few students were on campus and were still casting votes from their own devices as we had not set up any polling booth due to the pandemic restrictions. In the early evening hour of the polling day, we received a mail stating that a set of students who were the supporters of one of the Cultural Affairs Secretary (Literary) candidates, were involved in vote rigging at Zaitoon, erstwhile Anjappar. The then SEC Chief Commissioner Mr. Mihir Chawla, asked me and my coordinator to visit Anjappar and check the same. I went to the spot and identified the group of students who were sitting with laptops and phones and were constantly calling juniors to get their LDAP credentials and cast votes on their behalf. Understanding the gravity of the situation, I asked my coordinator to record the conversation that I would be having with them for the sake of evidence to safeguard myself if I were supposed to show it to any higher authority.

Without any second thought, I directly asked them to close their setup and leave Anjappar as they were performing malpractices of rigging votes and violating the constitutional clause of secrecy of votes. Within a few seconds, I was in a heated conversation with a group of 4 final year students who were cussing me in their native language. The moment they started abusing me in English I could not keep my calm and I too started retaliating in the same fashion for no reason. Till then, someone had called the Chief Election Commissioner and had asked him to arrive at the spot. The Chief arrived and made a settlement between me and the group and asked both of us to mind our respective businesses. But the stubborn Sushant inside me was still not ready to budge from that spot until or unless the recalcitrant group of students didn't leave that spot. After the incident, I along with Mihir and the coordinator were having tea at the Anjappar while the group gradually left the spot. By the time we reached our control room (present-day Career Development Cell's conference room), I got to know that I was going viral across Instagram for the act of bravery that I had shown as a representative of SEC to stop the vote rigging. Although it was a type of propaganda that the opposing identity group had initiated to defame the other candidate, indirectly SEC was getting all the praises for being active enough to act upon the complaint immediately. To have a detailed overview of this whole incident and SGE 2022, you all may watch this YouTube video titled *'IIT MADRAS College Elections! The Untold Side of IITs!'* made by SEC Coordinator Rahuram Chanthrakumar.[5]

That day, GSB realised the potential of SEC and I learned a lesson that inspired me to reach the zenith of SEC at all costs. Once the polling was over, I got a call from the DoST Office (Dean of Students' Office) asking me to be present for a DISCO (Disciplinary Committee) meeting at 7 PM the same day. Unaware of the consequences of DISCO, I sat in the DoST Office for 2 hours straight and shared the sofa with the same group of students with whom I had the verbal scuffle that day. Being oblivious to the DISCO meeting's consequences, one among the group of students asked me if I had launched a complaint against the incident to the DoST Office to which I said "No!". Puzzled about the complainant's identity, I also reciprocated the same question to them which they also denied. Unlike them, I was only worried about the quality time that I was losing by sitting idle in the office for such long hours. But those 4 boys were getting too anxious and were constantly whispering to each other. One by one each of us was called to the conference room, and I was the last one to be called in. By the time I was going to be invited to the conference room, all SEC Commissioners came in and went to the conference room without saying a word to me. While coming out of the conference room, one of those 4 boys was sobbing and seemed to be quite distressed. Unable to understand what is exactly happening around me, I also began to become anxious about the consequences of DISCO.

I went inside the conference room and saw the Chief Commissioner along with the DoST, Chief Election Officer, Election Officer, and Deputy Registrar who were looking at me with doubtful eyes. In the blink of a moment, the interrogation began which lasted for 30 minutes, and then I had to disprove all the false allegations that were imposed on me by the other students. After an intense conversation of half an hour, DoST Sir instructed me to be more careful from next time onwards and not to be too authoritative. He said "You all are students and are in the stage of learning, taking up such a PoR and regulating the students based on assumptions is very risky. First, always have concrete evidence in your hand and then peacefully try to engage with the students without creating much of a brawl around the campus." That day DoST Sir's words of wisdom were constraining my ego in all senses, but at a later point in time, his advice made sense to me. After 3 hours of grilling in the DoST Office, I realised my mistake, though a hard way but was determined enough to bring it into practice to seek my PoR salvation.

All three commissioners (Mr. Mihir Chawla, Ms. Ardra S. Shibu & Mr. Saket Saurabh) were empathetic enough to console me for whatever happened in the DoST Office and cheered me up for being innocent in this whole case. As we all were coming out of the office and moving towards Anjappar to have our dinner, Ardra suddenly asked me would you like to continue in the team further? She was expecting a negative response and was going to rejoice about it as she was fed up with the IITM administration and the team because of its unrewarding commitments. To her astonishment, I said "Absolutely Yes! I am going to become a Chief Commissioner and going to sit on the other side of the table in the upcoming DISCO meeting."

As per the Students' Constitution, the Chief Commissioner is the ex-officio member of all disciplinary committees that exist or going to be formed in the institute. Currently, there are 4 disciplinary committees in IITM - the Institute Disciplinary Committee for Students (IDCS), the Hostel Disciplinary Committee (HDC), the Disciplinary and Welfare Committee (DWC)/Academic Disciplinary Committee, and the Complaints Committee Against Sexual

Harassment (CCASH). HDC deals with all the disciplinary issues about the hostel, DWC deals with disciplinary issues about academics, disciplinary issues about sexual harassment are dealt with by CCASH and IDCS deals with all the other disciplinary issues. I am mentioning all these disciplinary committees here because, in the subsequent chapters, either of these committees will be mentioned now and then.

As mentioned before, after the Anjappar incident I was clear with my PoR ambitions and so was the institute because from the administration to students one thing was clear SEC has a lot of inbuilt potential in not just conducting elections but even in creating well-behaved future citizens of the country. That's where SECC comes into the picture.

Chapter 3

The Toothless Tiger - Commissioner (2022-2023)

The first stepping stone in becoming the Chief Commissioner of the SEC is to become the Commissioner of the Student Ethics and Constitution Commission (SECC) which I successfully did in June 2021. I still remember the question I could not answer during my interview: What is the impeachment process of the SECC Chief Commissioner? Little did I know that the same process would be witnessed by me in my Commissioner tenure which is the rarest of rare cases when it comes to SECC Commissioners. This is because, SECC Commissioners are recruited after rigorous scrutiny from not just the past commissioners but even by the newly elected SLC Speaker, SECC/SEC Faculty Advisor, and Dean of Students' Office. The nominated names for SECC Commissioners are then sent to the newly elected SLC to ratify (ratification of the new Chief Commissioner is done by the outgoing SLC), failing which the DoST ratifies them arbitrarily. On a final note of my interview, the former SECC Chief Commissioner Mihir advised me to not hold the position of Chief for more than one year. At first glance, it might look bewildering to you all as it did to me when I was applying for the position of SECC Commissioner. Still, seeing my potential and sensing my long-term ambition, Mihir cautioned me about the PoR lure that most students often fall into because of the habit of being in everyone's attention for a longer period.

My Chief Commissioner was Ms. Ardra S. Shibu and my co-commissioner was Ms. Alpha P. Jose with whom I had to test my naive ideas to bring SECC into the limelight. Out of the three commissioners I was the one who was agile enough to break the managerial inertia and watch out for opportunities every then and now. To begin with, I noticed a handful of issues within the organisation which I felt should be addressed at the earliest. First among them was to regain the dignity of SECC which it had lost in the eyes of administration due to the lack of interest from the latter. As mentioned before, the SECC Chief Commissioner is the ex-officio member of all the existing as well as upcoming disciplinary committees in the institute. However, for the past couple of years, SECC was no longer invited to any of the 4 aforementioned disciplinary committees due to the lack of reason behind making SECC part of such committees. Although these committees have student representatives like the Students' General Secretary (SGS), Hostel Affairs Secretary (HAS), Research Affairs Secretary (RAS) & Academic Affairs Secretary (AAS), none of them are well-versed with the Students' Constitution as SECC Commissioners are. To make the administration understand and abide by the Students' Constitution's simple clause, it took us around 3 months and the past commissions 2 years. Finally, my Chief started attending committees like IDCS, and in her absence, either my co-commissioner or I used to attend such committees. Our presence in the committee brought more pro-student angle arguments to the table which not only benefitted in improving the efficiency of IDCS but even the students in receiving reformative lessons.

Subsequently, I noticed that the number of cases that were filed with SECC often ranged from 1 to 2 and that too filed by the student government officials against each other. Two things I had mentioned to my co-commissioners were that there is a lack of awareness among GSB about SECC and its constitutional powers. Secondly, the methods of approaching SECC are very archaic, inefficient, and time-consuming. On the flip side of the coin, my co-commissioners felt that the second point was baseless as writing a mail is fairly a user-friendly process. However, to spread awareness about SECC among the GSB members, all commissioners along with the Heads of the Secretariat started devising new publicity and outreach methods like movie screening, periodic mail outreach, and so on. In our outreach email, the first half of it used to describe SECC while the second half was used to mention the Fundamental Rights that all GSB members are enshrined with. The only issue that was there with such publicity was that it seemed like smail (google group of all IITM students) spamming because the identity of the commissioners was always concealed in such emails. Not aware of the identity of the SECC Commissioners, earning students' trust was not just a challenge but even a nightmare because no one knew who the people operating behind the name of SECC were. However, we were still able to receive 3 to 4 complaints during our tenure which is a slight increase in comparison to the past commissions. Ardra used to mention to us that during her Commissioner tenure people used to file complaints only to SEC, and for the rest of the year, no one would be bothering them because no one used to file complaints to SECC.

I still remember, there was one case that had blown away my peace of mind and that was the unconstitutional removal of two team members by one of the executive council (EC) members in the year 2022. Before getting into the details of the case let me aware you of the broader political canvas on which this case was a mere stroke of paint. When a candidate wins the election to become one of the executive council members, the candidate is indebted to the backends (identity groups) that had helped her to win the elections. In most cases, the EC member would be awarding PoRs to only those students who are in her full support and are resonating from these particular backends. As there were no established rules for PoR recruitment until 2024, GSB members were often exploited by EC members under the umbrella of their Rulebooks which was not easily accessible to the GSB members. Making use of the constitutional illiteracy among the GSB members, the EC members at their wish used to recruit students whom they wanted to and used to fire students on frivolous grounds as per their whims and fancies. This not only promoted the idea of favoritism but even killed the spirit of meritocracy by allowing the EC members to abuse their powers. On the contrary, there were EC members who believed in the idea of meritocracy and evenly gave opportunities to all the GSB members to be part of their teams. But co-incidently such teams were having a majority of the students from the same identity group to which the EC member belonged.

One set of reasons is favoritism while the other set of reasons is limited access to PoR fundaes due to which the student bodies often used to be dominated by one of the identity groups. It is easy to understand that without even having the intention of favoritism, it is highly possible that the students from the same identity group can easily get PoRs because of early access to fundae sessions which are easily accessible in their native language. Getting to know the functioning of the teams in the early stage allows such students to outshine their competitors who might have got access to the fundaes only after the PoR applications were released. Moreover, GSB feels comfortable to work in a team if the leaders of the team speak the same language as them. Let me give you an example here, SECC 2022-23 was dominated by students (7/11 team members) who shared similar linguistic and regional backgrounds with my chief and co-commissioner. I am very well aware of the fact that my co-commissioners did not perform any favoritism while recruiting students for SECC PoRs as I was part of the process myself. However, with easy access to the SECC PoR fundaes our team had such a skewed demographic scenario that it became one of the reasons for citing Ardra's impeachment. The same was the scenario of SECC 2023-24 when I became the Chief Commissioner where there were 8/11 teammates from the Hindi-speaking background. From my experience, this skewed demographic composition is prevalent in every team of the institute may it be a constitutional body or an SGAO.

Coming back to the case, one of the EC members had fired two GSB members from his team on account of dereliction of duty and poor performance. When the students filed the complaint with us, we checked the constitutional validity of such an act as per the published Rulebook for that particular EC position. Then, we ordered the EC member to share the pieces of evidence and reports on the grounds on which he had fired the students as is mentioned in the due process of firing in the Rulebook. Failing to provide such pieces of evidence, the EC member questioned the authority of SECC itself and requested the intervention of DoST. DoST being the faculty advisor of the team, agreed to go ahead with the decision of the EC member irrespective of its ethicality. So that in the long run, the team can function well under the EC member without having any conflict of interest as the interest of the EC member was considered to be supreme over the constitutional rights of the team members. The DoST agreed to fire the students because these students have other PoRs where they can now function at their full potential. Sidelining the potential of the all-rounder students to save the face of the EC member not only brought injustice to those two students but even set a wrong precedence for the upcoming EC members. Being SECC Commissioners, we voiced our opinions consistently through the Chief who used to attend the meetings at the DoST Office but after some time, the Chief lost all hope and dropped the case. Finally, the EC member's whims and fancies were entertained and those two students had to face the brunt of injustice at a very high cost.

This case had set very bad precedence not just for the EC members but even for the administration. As they could meddle with SECC's functioning every then and now to favor the interests of the elected individuals (EC) at the behest of nominated individuals (SECC). This is because the EC was favored by the masses while the SECC was favored by the

Students' Constitution which the administration felt could be ignored to save the reputation of the administration and the EC members.

After this case, I understood the reason behind students' apathy in approaching SECC to seek justice as SECC was considered to be powerless in comparison to the EC members. This opinion was not just held by the students but even by the administration (like DoST) who often found negotiating with SECC easier than the EC members. Although, the Students' Constitution gave SECC the power to punish the guilty by (i) issuing a disciplinary warning (ii) suspending an individual or an organisation from a particular event for a particular period of time (iii) restricting someone from further participation or imposing fines (iv) seeking compensation for losses or (v) dismissing an elected representative. Still, SECC had no dignity in the eyes of either the GSB, EC members, or the administration because of its lenient attitude. This feeling of having the potential to do something but being unable to do it not only discouraged the commissioners to their core but was even brewing a skewed student government structure where EC was more powerful than SECC. I still recall the days when we commissioners often had to erupt our frustration over each other because of the nature of the work we were involved in where every piece of information was confidential and stressful.

On a deeper thought, we all commissioners realised one thing, the gender of the student government official plays an important role in the actions the official wants to implement. In an institute where the sex ratio is 9:1 which stands for every 9 boys there is 1 girl, gender neutrality is only on papers but not on the ground when it comes to the student politics of IIT Madras. Every year, there are only 1 or 2 female EC members who come into power because becoming an EC member in a male-dominated college is no less than a nightmare. I say this because I have seen the harassment that a female candidate has to go through when she is contesting in SGE. In the majority of the scenarios, the Gawds do not support the female candidates to contest for any EC position. This is because female candidates cannot be as casual as male candidates can be. Passing comments, cracking jokes, and roasting friends are more common attributes among boys than girls.

At the time of elections, female candidates would be offered deals by the Gawds so that they drop the idea of contesting the elections. Still, if the female candidates are strong enough to contest they are often the victim of mental harassment as they fall prey to threat calls, derogatory memes, and disturbing rumors. All this is intentionally done by the candidate preachers and mongers supporting the opposing male candidate to force the female candidates to drop their nominations. The surprising part of such acts is that such acts would never be formally reported to the SEC and the source of such actions will always remain anonymous. This is because the candidate preachers and mongers of the female candidate would perform the same actions to take revenge on the opposing candidates without seeking any formal assistance. This game of harassing each other keeps on going like a spiral and often ends up arousing vengeance against each other which is detrimental in the long run for the campus harmony. However, there were a handful of females who were brave enough to take up such challenges and outshine their competitors by winning the elections. Moreover, I do not solely blame the female candidates for not reporting such acts to the SEC but even hold the SEC responsible for not having any legal mechanism to deliver justice for digital harassment which females often used to face in the form of calls, memes or social media rumors.

There have been multiple such EC positions that have never been held by any female candidate to date, positions like SGS, SLC Speaker, AAS, and International & Alumni Relations Secretary (I&AR). Fortunately, SECC has been gender-neutral since its inception as it has witnessed female Chief Commissioners in every alternate year. This has been purely coincidental but rarely appreciated by anybody because a lot of people believe that female Chief Commissioners are not so efficient in comparison to male Chief Commissioners. I vehemently oppose this point of view and ardently highlight the positive aspect of having such a gender-neutral PoR which is rare to see in IITM. Ardra being a female Chief Commissioner, had to face a lot of issues not only from the students but even from the administration who used to turn deaf ears to her. One of the most, disrespectful acts that Ardra had to face during her Chief Commissioner tenure was the denial of a seat on the stage along with the EC members on the day of Institute Day (2023). Moreover, it was the same event where I was denied the honor that I should have been receiving for becoming the next Chief Commissioner of SECC for the academic year 2023-24. In short, both Ardra and I were denied to be part of the Investiture Ceremony (2023) which marks a significant moment for not just SECC but even for the GSB members as they get to know their student government officials in a better manner.

All this happened because of the indifferent administration and an overambitious Gawd turned student government official who used to play the victim card of his caste identity in such a manner that it handcuffed the administration from taking any stringent step against his recalcitrant attitude. A student wanted to become a student government official for the academic year 2022-23 and was ambitious to make IITM student politics similar to institutes like JNU. Unable to contest in the elections due to his personal (Gawd) commitments to his juniors, he decided to get nominated as the Financial Accountability Committee (FAC) Chairperson by any hook and crook to become part of the student government. Even without following the proper constitutional mandate, the student proclaimed himself as the Chairperson of FAC (a constitutional body of IIT Madras) which remained unchecked by both the then-student government as well as the administration. All this could happen because the then SLC Speaker was a good friend of this Gawd who had the sole authority to recruit the members of FAC, a constitutional body that had been dormant for the past couple of years.

We the custodians of the Students' Constitution were well aware of this scenario and were repeatedly writing to both the student government and the administration to refrain from entertaining him at any cost. Neither of them gave heed to us until the self-proclaimed FAC Chairperson became an impediment to the fruitful functioning of the STACT

Office[6*] and the SLC. As per the Students' Constitution, the FAC has the mandate to audit the budget and investigate the financial misappropriation of the student government bodies or SGAOs. In no manner, does FAC have the mandate to audit or investigate the IITM administration's financial documents. However, the FAC started cross-checking the confidential sponsorship documents that the Institute or the EC members had signed with the outside parties to make it public which it shouldn't. As per the constitution, DoST is the faculty advisor of FAC whose sole role is to advise FAC and be briefed by FAC regarding the financial health of the student government. In this case, the DoST was unhappy with the functioning of the FAC Chairperson and was reluctant to help FAC at all stages of its investigations. Fed up with the indifferent attitude of DoST, the FAC Chairperson approached SECC to which SECC replied about his unconstitutional position and his subsequent unconstitutional actions. Seeing our dismissive response not only frustrated him but even led him to develop envy against our Chief Commissioner - Ardra at the professional level. Simultaneously, the legislators from the SLC were constantly complaining to us regarding the FAC Chairperson's interventions which was disturbing the peaceful decorum of SLC every then and now. In response to their complaints, SECC reminded the SLC Speaker of his responsibilities and asked him to maintain decorum in the SLC during all the sessions.

[6*] STACT Office is part of the IITM DoST Office which refers to the Students Activities Trust that is enshrined with the responsibility of dispensing funds for student related activities.

With periodic tussles between FAC Chairperson and SECC Commissioners, Ardra was frustrated with him and didn't want to cooperate with him at any cost. During the SGE 2023 when the FAC Chairperson was constantly calling her to get insider information regarding the final nomination list, Ardra erupted over him with all her anger. This initiated the spark of vengeance in the FAC Chairperson against her which initially led her to impeachment and finally to the denial of a seat on the day of Institute Day. Though both events are unrelated the source of such events was the revenge that the FAC Chairperson always wanted to take from Ardra. At the time of SGE 2023, the FAC Chairperson had initiated the impeachment process against Ardra on the grounds of showing favoritism to the alike identity group candidates and discriminating against the Hindi-speaking candidates. He also accused her of non-performance of duties as mentioned in the Students' Constitution and had received the support of at least 20 legislators at the time of initiating the impeachment process.[7*]

Everyone in the SEC team from Election Officers to the Head of Secretariats knew that all the allegations were false and were spuriously levied to achieve the frivolous interests of the FAC Chairperson and his associated backend. Ardra was in a state of depression and was not in the right state of mind to defend herself in front of the biased SLC where she had to face public ignominy. For the betterment of Ardra and SEC, the Election Officers decided to send me to the SLC as her spokesperson as I had neutral relations with everyone in the

---

[7*] The Section VII of the Students' Constitution elaborately mentions about the impeachment process of the SECC Commissioner.

student government. Looking at the gravity of the situation (impeaching the Chief Election Commissioner during the Elections) and the meager possibility of successfully impeaching Ardra, the SLC Speaker decided to drop the impeachment process as it required at least three-fourths of the total legislators' vote in favor of the motion.

A few hours before the Investiture ceremony, I still remember the multiple emails that we had written to DoST cautioning him about his indifferent attitude towards SECC for Institute Day because of the illegitimate demand of the FAC Chairperson. Being the head of a constitutional body, the FAC Chairperson wished to share the seat along with the EC as the SECC Chief Commissioner (head of another constitutional body) used to sit on the stage on Institute Day along with the EC members. The DoST didn't want to agree to the demand of the FAC Chairperson and so he decided to remove SECC, The Fifth Estate (T5E)[8*], MITR, and Centre for Innovation (CFI)[9*] Heads from the stage except the EC members. The DoST didn't want to agree to the FAC Chairperson's demand because he had started writing false emails to higher authorities like the National Minority Commission and media houses stating that he was being discriminated against by the institute because he belonged to a minority category. He was adamant enough to not accept his mistake of not following the Students' Constitution and had made false allegations against the institute of caste discrimination. To subjugate the FAC Chairperson, the

---

8* T5E is the official media body of IIT Madras that gained its legitimacy from the Students' Constitution.

9* Centre for Innovation is the India's largest 24x7 student run innovation lab.

DoST had to treat the organisations like SECC, T5E, MITR, and CFI below their established stature to maintain peace and harmony in the institute. Although the DoST was able to subjugate the false allegations of the FAC Chairperson it came at the cost of the aforementioned teams who had been putting their heart and souls for the greater good of the GSB.

Unfortunately, Ardra had to face all this because of the banal acts of a student government official who preferred to achieve accolades by using his caste identity rather than serving the GSB selflessly. Unlike Ardra who had been serving the GSB for the past 2 years by being part of the SECC first as the Commissioner and then as the Chief Commissioner.

This was the same period when the conflict between the two identity groups rose to prominence purely based on region and language. These two identity groups were the Northies and the Malus who turned into enemies on one odd morning of 15th February 2023. After celebrating the prom night at the Student Activity Centre (SAC) a group of Malu boys went to D'Diet (a tea shop near the Taramani IITM Gate) to sip a cup of tea. At the same place, the SLC Speaker arrived along with his friends (drunk) after attending a party in a nearby restobar. Recalling the email thread that was initiated by the SLC Speaker about wasting GSB's money on a handful of students' enjoyment by conducting prom night only for couples, the Malus were having a fun time giggling among themselves. The SLC Speaker (a Hindi speaker) unable to make sense of the Malu's conversation, got up from his chair and started arguing with the Malus for no reason. With time, the verbal argument turned into a physical fight but was somehow hushed by the locals around. Filled with ego and pride about their identities, both parties chose to sit in D'Diet until one of them didn't leave that place. Later in the morning of 15th February 2023, the Northies started marching towards the Taramani gate and after some time even Malus left D'Diet and moved towards the gate. Little did they know that they were going to get beaten by a larger Northie mob who were armed with hockey sticks and were enchanted by their seniors that the Malus had molested a Northie girl. The mob consisted of Northies' campaign mongers and preachers who were blindly following the command of their Gawd and had arrived outside the Taramani gate to fight with Malus to take revenge for molesting a Northie girl. By now you all would have understood that Northie Gawds had spread a rumour to agitate their backend to satisfy their ego and no act of molesting had taken place the previous night. It was a one-sided fight that happened exactly opposite the Taramani gate where the Malus were brutally beaten by the Northies and the Malus could do nothing about it.

Later in the day, when I saw my Malu classmates with bruises on their bodies and their friends approaching me to seek advice about the future proceedings. I was astounded by the foolishness with which IITM students had started behaving under the guise of their identity which was turning out to be detrimental to the campus harmony. This fight was the source of a major conflict that was still to come in the upcoming days of the SGE 2023. After taking my advice, one of the Malu students decided to file a complaint with the IDCS about the Taramani gate incident. The IDCS did not take the case up for further investigation as the incident had happened outside the institute boundary and hence IDCS outrightly rejected the complaint.

Tired of seeking justice through formal methods of filing complaints, the agony among Malus against Northies was brewing for the apt moment to take revenge for the Taramani gate incident. This agony of Malus finally erupted at the time of the AAS Soapbox where there were only two candidates, one being Malu and the other being Northie. Throughout the elections, the AAS position was the center of attraction for everyone as it gave Malus a chance to lacerate Northies for every mistake that the Northie candidate made during the elections. On the day of AAS Soapbox, there was three times more the number of audience than we had expected as part of the SEC. Unaware of the dangerous strategies that these groups were devising against each other before the AAS soapbox. SEC was in a disadvantageous position as it could not foresee the drama that was going to unfold on a YouTube livestream that was viewed by hundreds of viewers across the world. During the AAS soapbox when the Northie candidate was unable to answer a question, someone from the crowd shouted *"Northies are the most foolish set of people"*. When the Malu candidate was cheering, one among the agitated Northies tore the poster that was held by the Malu supporter in the crowd. With the tearing of the poster, a communal fight erupted in the crowd which was telecasted live on YouTube, maligning the reputation of IITM in front of the whole world. Without hesitation, the Malus used this opportunity to take revenge on the Northies for the Taramani gate incident, which had been making Malus restless for a long time.

With the advent of the IITM Police, the students were dispersed from the SAC, and a handful of them were hospitalised in the institute hospital on an emergency basis. The communal fight was brutal enough to hospitalise students from both groups and bring this incident right under the immediate attention of the DoST. The same night, DoST called for an immediate meeting with the SEC and passed orders to form an ad-hoc disciplinary committee to investigate this incident carefully.

The ad-hoc disciplinary committee consisted of the former IDCS Chairperson, former Election Officers, Chief Security Officer, and SECC Commissioners who collectively investigated the AAS Soapbox Conflict in 5 days and submitted the report to DoST to take the required action. Because it was a communal fight, spotting the exact faces was a challenge for the committee. As per the investigation, no one knew how the fight started but everyone knew that in the act of self-defense, they had to be part of this fight. Secondly, students from both identity groups mentioned that the other group had used hockey sticks during the fight. The Malus consistently brought up the Taramani gate incident as the reason behind the fight while the Northies brought the loose comment passed during the soapbox as the reason behind the fight. The committee submitted a detailed report to DoST to take stringent actions against the students who were involved in the fight. In the list of the students, there was a mention of the FAC Chairperson as well due to which the DoST chose not to give any stringent punishments to the students and decided to give all these students a verbal reprimand. The rationale behind DoST's decision was to avert the caste politics that the FAC Chairperson could have invoked if he or his friends had been punished. From the day of the AAS Soapbox, all the subsequent soapboxes were conducted in an online manner. However, the lenient attitude of the DoST now encouraged the backends to do something bolder without fearing the SEC or the administration for their selfish gains.

As the campaigning period was going to come to an end, a few of the incumbent EC members approached DoST with the demand to postpone the Polling Day as the candidates needed more time to campaign. Unconvinced by the arguments of the incumbent EC members, the DoST outrightly rejected their demands. This is a particular point in time when all the backends came together to put forward their demands to the IITM administration to bypass the SEC's election schedule. The same day, the EC members along with the FAC Chairperson approached the Director with their demand at 7 PM. The Director being altruistic and student-friendly agreed to their demand and called DoST, Election Officers, and SEC Commissioners for a meeting at 8 PM at his office. Without giving heed to any of our arguments, the Director instructed us to postpone the Polling Date and increase the campaigning period for the ease of the GSB as the current campaigning period got compromised due to the postponement of Quiz 1. My Chief was absolutely against the will of the Director and was not willing to agree to his instructions as she felt the autonomy of SEC was getting compromised. Since I was the only SEC commissioner present along with Ardra, I tried to convince the Director about its dire consequences but finally adhered to his instructions due to his overarching authority. As soon as we got out of the Director's Office, Ardra was in a very bad shape of mind and was constantly sobbing as she felt that SEC had lost all its autonomy under her tenure.

She was disturbed by this incident to such an extent that she decided to resign from her post if she was forced to accept the postponement of the polling day. DoST Sir along with the Election Officers were trying to console Ardra and were asking her to not take any action emotionally. Seeing her so much distressed for the first time, I decided to call Alpha and the former SECC Commissioner Saket Saurabh to console Ardra and refrain her from resigning from her post. On the other hand, I had a Microeconomics Quiz 1 the next day but I had chosen to stay with my team near the Cafe Coffee Day (CCD) at 10 PM that night. After discussing the possible solutions that we as a team could undertake (ranging from mass resignation to postponing Polling Day), all 11 people were patient enough to stay with us till 1 AM. Looking at the frail state of Ardra, I requested her classmates to take good care of her in the hostel. With 2 hours of sleep and quick skimming through the 9 chapters, I decided to write Quiz 1 with all my confidence. Even though the course instructor of the course was Prof. Anup Kumar Bhandari, he was the faculty advisor of the SECC who knew me and my condition very well. I chose to not be lenient on myself and decided to write the Quiz with whatever last-minute revision I could do.

Stressed about my academic commitments, I chose to let them loose a bit to find a solution to the Director's instructions. One thing was clear to me if we resigned from our posts today it would validate the wrongdoings of the backend and would compromise the autonomy of SEC further. Analysing the gravity of the situation, I reached out to all the EC members and convened an online meeting to discuss the possible date of a polling day. After considering their demands I suggested a new date which gave enough time for the candidates to campaign around the campus and SEC the required time to make arrangements for the polling day. Unlike any other SGE, SGE 2023 under the leadership of Ardra deployed India's first Blockchain-based Voting Portal that was built by the Webops and Blockchain Club of CFI which was the biggest contribution to IITM by SEC to date.[6] Finally, the SGE 2023 came to an end and the aforementioned incidents of the Institute Day happened even after the remarkable achievements of SEC under the able leadership of Ardra.

Although I did receive an invitation to the Institute Day not for becoming the next SECC Chief Commissioner but for being the batch topper of the Humanities and Social Sciences department for the academic year 2021-22. That day, I was awarded the Institute Merit Award by the Director but not any recognition for becoming the next Chief Commissioner. I was partially sad about the fact that I could not become one of those rare student government officials who are academically sound and PoR-wise strong. More than me, Ardra was sad about me as she felt that I never had the chance of getting recognised as the Chief Commissioner in front of the GSB as she got it in the year 2022.

Taking a pledge to myself, I had made up my mind that I was going to regain the lost glory of SECC & SEC during my tenure and was going to earn the recognition that an SECC Commissioner should get in an eminent institute like IIT Madras.

Struggling to cope with her mental health and academic burden, Ardra chose to perform her duties sincerely by the end of her tenure. She wrote to the SLC Speaker to ratify me as the new SECC Chief Commissioner but the SLC Speaker chose not to propose this agenda in the upcoming SLC sessions to hamper the functioning of SECC. Before I could act upon my ratification, the tenure of SLC Speaker of 2022-23 was exhausted and my ratification remained incomplete.

Before embarking on this challenging journey of being the SECC Chief Commissioner, I recalled Sun Tzu's famous quote "Victory comes from finding opportunities in problems". Being aware of the cunning attitude of the SLC Speaker and the indifferent persona of the DoST. I decided to put a humble request to DoST before starting my tenure that the DoST Office should circulate an email announcing the SECC Commissioners for the academic year 2023-24 as they do for the EC members. Seeing no harm in my request, the DoST immediately accepted my request and asked me to inform the DoST Office once SECC Commissioners are recruited.

Initially, as the CMOH, I understood the SEC's potential, later as the Commissioner I understood the SECC's potential. It was now the right time to expand and exploit the potential of both SECC and SEC by acting as the 7th Chief Commissioner of IIT Madras and leaving a revolutionary mark for the institute to remember forever.

Chapter 4

The Golden Age - Chief Commissioner (2023-2024)

I address my Chief Commissioner tenure as the golden age not because I was living my dream but because SECC & SEC were out of the pipe dream after a long-drawn struggle. This was when I chose to revolutionise the whole bureaucratic organisation by taking a big leap into nurturing social and political etiquette among GSB as a long-term investment. I took up the post of Chief Commissioner intending to achieve the 3Ts - Transparency, Technological Inclusiveness, and Trust for the betterment of the GSB and the welfare of the institute. By Transparency, I meant making the GSB aware of what SECC has been doing by publishing periodic reports about its completed, ongoing, and upcoming tasks. By Technological Inclusiveness I meant to deploy technology to bring SECC & SEC one step closer to the GSB first and then the world around. By Trust, I meant the faith the GSB, administration, and everyone around us should have in SECC & SEC to build meaningful relationships that mutually benefit everyone. To turn all my promises into accomplishments, I had to have a team willing to work with the same vigor and dedication as I was willing to work.

For the position of SECC Commissioner, there were 3 applicants out of which I had chosen only one student as the other two did not meet my eligibility standards. My eligibility standards were high not because of my ego but because of the selfless commitment that I was expecting from the Commissioners for the welfare of the GSB. In the past, I have seen Chiefs who used to recruit Commissioners to fill the positions by compromising on the quality. I was a Chief who gave priority to quality and was willing to head the team even with 2 Commissioners instead of having 3. With only 1 co-commissioner, Ardra cautioned me about the heavy workload while SECC's Faculty Advisor Prof. Anup Kumar Bhandari alerted me about the dire need for a third opinion at the time of conflict of opinions between two Commissioners. Keeping everyone's advice in mind, I chose to start my journey with only one Commissioner on the team and was ready to face any challenge that came my way because I was vouching for such challenges.

Ms. Tejaswini Jagtap was my co-commissioner who not only met my eligibility standards but was witty enough to make bold decisions. Our first step was to bring SECC into the limelight by earning the trust of the GSB members. To make this happen, we changed our rudimentary approach from students approaching SECC to SECC approaching students for help. We started sending publicity emails every fortnight to the GSB about the fundamental rights and grievance redressal mechanism that the Students' Constitution had guaranteed them. Simultaneously we devised new methods of filing complaints by creating a separate tab on the menu page of the *InstiSpace App* titled - 'Complaints to SECC'.[7] With just a few clicks, students could now reach out to SECC with their grievances and they could get live updates about their complaints. On a macro scale, we had initiated the creation of the SECC website which not only allowed students to file complaints with us but even allowed them to visit the repository of past cases that were resolved by SECC since its inception (18 cases have been solved until April 2024).[8] Within one semester we received 7 cases which was more than the total number of cases that the past commissions in totality had solved until 2023.

The SECC Website was a big leap forward as it not only allowed the students to file complaints but even allowed them to get real-time updates about the status of their complaints. Moreover, the website is used as the medium to communicate our upcoming events ranging from Elections to SECC events. The website also became a one-stop solution for people outside IITM to know about the student politics of the No. 1 educational institute of India from the most neutral point of view as it is the SECC that manages the whole website. All this could not have been possible without the technical assistance of Arun Sir and his team, who have acted as the shield of SEC for the past 3 years. I say this because earlier we used to make our nomination and voting portal using the services of a third party who used to charge us around 2 lakhs. On the contrary, Arun Sir used to charge us a nominal fee (below 1 lakh) and cater to our real-time needs even at the last moment. I am mentioning all these facts not at their face value but to make you all realise that until 2024 the student politics of IIT Madras has been archaic enough to stick to inefficient methods of governance. There is no other student government official or team that periodically publishes about its completed, ongoing, and upcoming tasks. The level of transparency that is expected from a student government official is not even at its bare minimum at IIT Madras. In fact, as per *Chapter IV, Section II, Clause III* of the Students' Constitution all the EC members are supposed to submit a report every 2 months to the SLC detailing the actions so far taken and planning to take during their term.

Honestly, I wanted to impose sanctions on all the EC members including SLC for not abiding by this constitutional law. However, SECC itself did not follow this law due to which I had to reform my team policies first and then had to encourage others to follow the same. From my tenure onwards I started publishing the SECC Newsletter by the end of every semester so that the EC members too gradually imitate the same.

On the other hand, students are very reluctant to take financial accountability for the expenses that their team shall undertake during the year. Most of the student government officials prefer to amplify their team budget to earn their respective 'cuts' which in literal terms can be understood as 'black money'. I can firmly say that SEC is one of those organisations that has never executed such corrupt practices and has always attempted to use an appropriate amount of students' money with full sincerity. Just because students are paying money to the institute, we student government officials do not have the sole right to exploit it as per our wish. The most basic level of financial misappropriation that happens in the institute is done by the hostel secretaries. Each hostel has a semester budget of around 5 lakh rupees or above and there are 7 secretaries in a hostel council. At the time of procurement of goods from the vendors, the hostel secretaries would often ask for an inflated bill (say a bill of ₹20,000 would be printed as ₹30,000) with a deal that 40% of the inflation difference (₹4000) shall be under the table given to the salesman. The rest of the amount shall remain with the secretary or shall be distributed among the 7 of them. This has been communicated to me by the Hostel Wardens who have caught many hostel secretaries red-handed when I was the Chief Commissioner. It is usually said that by the end of their term, every hostel secretary earns around 50 thousand and above through such corrupt practices. Now just imagine how much would EC members be earning as they deal with a budget of 10 lakhs and above.

Such corrupt acts are normal to surface in an institute like IITM where constitutional bodies like FAC (Financial Accountability Committee) are non-functional because of the whims and fancies of the SLC Speakers. I believe that the quality of the student government depends on the quality of the SLC Speaker. For the past 3-4 years, applications for the post of FAC members have not been released, and if released one semester would have passed by. The same is the case with a committee called NARC (Nomination and Ratification Committee) which used to be formed at least 4 months after the convening of the 1st session of SLC until 2023. The purpose of ratification is to gain public legitimacy and mark the official starting point of the tenure. The SLC Speaker in association with the EC members used to ratify the student government officials (SECC Commissioners) and PoR holders only 4 months after assuming their positions so that

SECC becomes handicapped and PoR holders could be fired at ease without taking any accountability by the EC members (as happened in 2022-23). SECC becoming handicapped means that SECC has 3 commissioners in totality out of which at least 2 of them have not been ratified for SECC to function. Other than the Chief Commissioner, the other two Commissioners used to get ratified 4 months after assuming their positions. This allowed the student and the EC members to question the validity of SECC's authority if SECC used to regulate their actions before getting ratified.

The same was attempted with my commission too, aware of this dirty politics, I had raised this point during my Commissioner tenure when the case of unlawful removal of the two students from a team had come up. The EC member was able to defend himself in front of the administration and the student government only because those two students were not ratified in the SLC. Since those students were not ratified in the SLC, the EC member was not obligated to submit any evidence for their removal to SECC which we had demanded from him. We commissioners (SECC 2022-23) brought this point to the table of DoST to which he responded that since Faculty Advisors ratify their teams at the time of recruitment, the students shall start performing their duties the moment they assume positions without bothering about SLC's ratification. The SLC can take its own legitimate time to form NARC and later ratify these students.

To stall my actions, one of the EC members used the ratification argument against me and Tejaswini which was thwarted by DoST's aforementioned statement all at once. I am talking about a case that not only brought me and

Tejaswini to everyone's attention but even allowed SECC to build a perception that was going to change the fate of SECC forever. One month passed after the new EC members had assumed their positions, one of the EC members introduced a new club under his SGAO. As per the Students' Constitution, to introduce any new club the EC member has to first get it passed in the SLC and then he can release the application forms to fill the position of Heads, Super-Coordinators & Coordinators in that club. That particular EC member had released the application form directly on the smail without even proposing the club in the SLC. As SECC Commissioners, me and Tejaswini decided to take a *suo moto* cognisance of this particular incident and we issued a Writ of Prohibition on the smail. The EC member enraged by this act of SECC chose to ignore SECC's writ and decided to send a mail from the SGAO's account (mentioning the names of SGAO Heads) stating that the applications are open. As an act of Contempt of Court, we punished the EC member (along with the SGAO Heads) with the harshest of sanctions given to SECC by the Students' Constitution. We suspended the EC member for 24 hours and withdrew his official mailing access. Such a bold act spread like wildfire all across the institute and by the end of the day, everyone in the institute including the administration was shocked by this incident. At this point, I would again like to appreciate the boldness of Tejaswini who with all her integrity supported me and imposed sanctions on SGAO Heads as well who were her friends. Feeling the brunt of the Commissioner position early in her career with such a difficult case was not an easy decision for her.

Unable to act as per his will, the EC member reached out to DoST for help and asked him to coerce us to take back our sanctions. The same evening I received a call from Prof. Anup Kumar Bhandari and he communicated to me the request of DoST Sir which I firmly denied. After the completion of the 24 hours I gave the EC member his mailing access back and in retaliation, he removed our mailing access. When we informed the same to the DoST and the Computer Centre Chairperson, they said that the mail moderation rights are totally under the purview of the EC members and they can only grant access. Realising the upper hand that was given to the EC members over the mail moderation rights, gave me another opportunity to keep the powers of the EC under check.

Removing the mail moderation access for SECC would have clearly shown the envious intent of the EC member so he decided to remove the mail moderation access of all the nominated Heads. These nominated Heads are none other than the MITR Head, T5E Chief Editor, CFI Head & SECC Commissioners whom I collectively used to address as MITACS. This was the same time when Prof. Sathyanarayana N. Gummadi was appointed as the DoST of IIT Madras. He asked MITACS to give a detailed presentation about their respective teams and asked us to forward all the concerns that we had. We as MITACS collectively voiced our opinion regarding the access to mail moderation right for which he created a Mail Moderation Committee. Till then I as the SECC Chief Commissioner had periodic meetings with the EC members and came to a negotiation that no one shall be moderating SECC emails. Making use of the divide-and-rule policy among the EC members I got 6 for votes and 3 against votes for the proposal and finally got my partial mail moderation access back.

Simultaneously we had also demanded to be part of the Board of Students (BoS) which we earlier were but due to the ego of a few EC members, the BoS had been solely attended by the EC members and chaired by the DoST. The presence of nominated Heads like SECC is important in such boards as any bill or constitutional amendment that gets passed in SLC has to get passed through BoS and subsequently in the Senate. A board dominated by elected individuals will not only lead to the propagation of majoritarianism but will often lead to unscrupulous decisions like it happened in the case of bifurcation of SECC. In the year 2022, the SLC passed the proposal that they were going to bifurcate SECC and SEC into two separate organisations without even consulting SECC Commissioners. As the proposal reached the BoS in 2023, SECC could not defend it but luckily as few EC members were in favor of SECC the proposal was stalled and it did not reach the Senate. The Senate is the highest body in the institute that is responsible for the maintenance of standards of instruction, education, and examination in the institute. It is composed of professors and is chaired by the Director, only three student representatives SGS, RAS & AAS are allowed to attend the Senate. Later, DoST made all the nominated Heads part of BoS as the invitees, and since then we have been invited to the BoS as and when required.

Coming back to the mail moderation case, now I had the right to send direct emails to the GSB without seeking any EC members' permission. However, in the future, if I had to suspend any EC member then too I should have the mail moderation right over and above the EC members. This right was granted to us by the Mail Moderation Committee later during my tenure which stated that SECC first had to prepare a ruling for removing some EC's mail moderation rights and then had to send it to DoST and Computer Centre for the execution of the ruling. After streamlining the mail moderation policy for SECC, now it was time for the SEC to sort its mail moderation right which I realised during the Special Election 2023. On the day of the polling of the Special Election of the Institute Sports Secretary (ISS), one of the backends had sent a defamatory mail against the opposing candidate (Tams) to gain more votes for his Northie candidate. Unapologetically the mail was approved by one of the EC members and it led to havoc in the institute. As SEC Commissioners we took a *suo motu* cognisance and filed a complaint against the student as well as the EC member for violating the Model Code of Conduct. On further investigation, we found out the EC member and sent him a written reprimand for such an irresponsible act. This allowed me to separately form a mail moderation policy during SGE 2024 where I revoked the mail moderation rights of all the EC members for 48 hours beginning from one day before the polling day.

One thing to note here is that Special Elections are different from Students' General Elections as the former happens only when an elected member resigns from her post or the post remains vacant after following Annexure I & Annexure IV of the Election Manual. The upcoming SGE should be at least three months away from the point of time when the elected position is vacant. After fulfilling these two conditions, the Special Elections for ISS were conducted as the former ISS had resigned from his post. Again, I am the only Chief who has conducted the first Special Elections of IIT Madras. In short, I conducted two SGEs in one year because, in the ISS Special Elections 2023, the whole institute voted. I would term that Special Election as a blessing in disguise because it not only cautioned me about the possible shortcomings of SGE but made the actual SGE a cake for me and my team.

The second way in which the ISS Special Election (along with the Freshers' Elections) was a boon for me was to revoke a Constitutional Crisis created by SLC. The crisis was a result of a decision that was motivated by vengeance but not by constitutional logic. The same EC member was so jealous of me that at the time of ratification, he made a student file a complaint against me and my co-commissioner to the NARC. The complaint stated that without getting ratified, Tejaswini and I had been acting as the SECC Commissioners from day one. Because we were performing our duties as Commissioners before getting ratified hence we should not be ratified. Since the SLC Speaker was on good terms with the EC member he took up the complaint and formed an ad-hoc committee that presented a report about the same. The ad-hoc committee did not find any unconstitutionality in our actions (one of them being conducting ISS Special Election and Freshers' Elections 2023) and accordingly mentioned it in its report. However, the report was tabled in the SLC and surprisingly it was put to vote which was constitutionally invalid. Here comes the interesting part, at the time of voting there was that specific EC member who saw that the legislators were voting in favor of ratifying us. During the voting, he began to yell at the top of his voice "We cannot ratify those people who are not student-friendly and use constitutional powers to regulate GSB rather than facilitating them!". As soon as he triggered the legislators, many of them changed their votes to against and hence we were not ratified. Before leaving the session I chose to just ask one question openly to the SLC "Can anyone tell me under which section of the Constitution did you all vote against me and my commissioner?". Not even a single hand rose to answer my question and I understood that SLC is now literally into a Constitutional Crisis.

Not everything was gloomy in that particular session, among the 3 of us it was only Ms. Meenakshi Anoop who was an SLC-ratified SECC Commissioner. Before I tell you more about Meenakshi, let me complete the story about ratification first. We reported about this instance to our new Faculty Advisor Prof. Anbarasu Manivannan who was the former Chief Election Officer of IIT Madras. Prof. Anbarasu reported the incident to the DoST and the DoST formed an ad-hoc committee chaired by former DoST Prof. Nilesh J. Vasa. The committee found that I and my co-commissioner have not performed any unconstitutional acts and are not being ratified because of personal and political reasons. Hence, the committee quashed the SLC's decision and framed a new law stating that if the SLC fails to ratify the Commissioners on time then the DoST shall ratify them arbitrarily. After the Constitutional Crisis was over, I remember I had sent an email to the GSB stating that the SECC had successfully delivered justice to 54 legislators by resolving the Constitutional Crisis on the day of New Year's Eve.

The only Commissioner in SECC 2023-24 getting ratified by SLC was Meenakshi who is yet a very street smart lady but is equally good at analysing any situation from myriad perspectives. While I was busy with the RBI Internship in Chennai and dealing with the EC member's suspension, I received a call on one odd evening from one of my fellow juniors from the HS21 batch. That fellow junior of mine was none other than Ms. Meenakshi whom I had never met earlier on the campus. But she called me to take fundaes for the position of CMOH for which she was going to apply. Within a 15-minutes of conversation, I sensed her strengths and based on that, I encouraged her to apply for the position of SECC Commissioner as her demeanor is more perfect for the role of Commissioner than any other role. She took my advice seriously and she applied for the position of SECC Commissioner along with 2 other candidates who were now desperate to become part of SECC. This is because all the EC members were trying to make one of their friends the SECC Commissioner so that they could get the insider information at ease. Especially the Northie backend because I and Tejaswini already resonated with Northies because of our social background, having one more Northie Commissioner would allow the Northie backend to prove their dominance over other backends. But Meenakshi being Meenakshi was witty enough to outshine all her competitors and joined my team at a time when the Freshers' and ISS Special Elections 2023 were just going to be conducted in a few weeks.

Both my Commissioners or rather say *Devis* were perfect complements of each other as Tejaswini was good at making bold decisions, and Meenakshi was good at analysing a situation from myriad angles. My job was to make the best use of their synergy, work shoulder-to-shoulder with them, and give directions to the whole team. Even though, Meenakshi joined the team 3 months later than the conception of the commission her fantastic work ethic allowed her to ace the ladder of succession and become the Chief Commissioner of SECC 2024-25. As a matter of fact in the academic year 2023-24, among the top brass people of the student government, only these two *Devis* were females. Rest everyone was male spanning from SECC Chief Commissioner to EC & SLC Speaker.

The first case that was solved by all three commissioners was a case similar to the 2023 case of the unethical removal of the two students from a team by the EC member. The EC member thought that just like his former EC member he would also be able to get out of this trouble with DoST's help. However, in this case, both the students were ratified unlike in the 2023 case and both of them had been unlawfully removed from the team without following the Rulebook. The case went on for 29 days and finally, the DoST supported our argument and asked the EC member to reinstate both those students respectfully in his team. The longest case that I have ever dealt with spanned 72 days which involved financial misappropriation by an EC member for which an ad-hoc committee was set up by the DoST. The committee was headed by the SECC Faculty Advisor Prof. Anbarasu and a corruption of around ₹40,000 was estimated. However, due to a lack of evidence and the over-defensive attitude of the Faculty Advisor of that EC member, the case was dissolved.

One of the most difficult cases of my life was the case related to the Parliament Trip which happened at the time of end-semester exams. Although I have dealt with many other worst situations during the end-semester exams earlier in my SECC career, the Parliament Trip case of 2023 was one of the most challenging cases for me. At this point, one of my commissioners was not in a position to work because of her health commitments while the other was too stressed about the exams so I asked her to focus on her exams first and gave her temporary leave. There were around 8 to 10 cases filed against the SLC Speaker and his SGAOs for inappropriately conducting the selection procedure for the contingent that was going to be taken for the Parliament Trip. As per the complaints, GSB members who were selected in the majority were either the Hindi-speaking students or were the friends of the Speaker and his organising team. In short, the contingent had a skewed representation of the students of IITM due to which the purpose that the Parliament Trip was going to serve seemed to be doubtful. After a deep inquiry into the selection procedure, I along with the 3 other EC members concluded that there isn't any apparent discrimination in the selection process. However, we recommended a few additional selections of students from selected departments and programs with negligible representation in the contingent. Based on the same report, the SLC Speaker 2024-25 was advised to devise a policy that solves the issue of the Parliament Trip forever.

After solving at least 8 cases, I felt that the mental health of the students who are involved in the case often gets compromised to a very significant extent. To look after their mental health, we commissioners collaborated with MITR and the Wellness Centre and started attaching a pamphlet that had all the helpline numbers to deal with the same.

Simultaneously, I felt that since the GSB is the supreme power in the Students' Constitution, they should have the right to give meaningful feedback to us once the case is over. So I integrated a feedback section in the SECC website which allowed the parties to give their feedback once the cases were closed. All these reforms came to my mind after I witnessed a handful of protests in the institute which was the result of the deteriorated mental health of the students.

In the year 2023, there were approximately 4 suicide attempts out of which 3 turned out to be fatal and the students were declared dead. It was such a horrible year for IITM that the students believed in rumors more than facts. A suicide is never caused by one factor, it is a product of multiple factors out of which one of the factors triggers the student to commit suicide. In such a stressful environment, students of all identity groups stand united and seek justice for the deceased students by conducting protests in the GC (Gajendra Circle). As per the Students' Constitution, GSB is allowed to protest within the hostel zone, so all the backends join hands to lead the protest against the administration. All such protests aim to seek responses from the administration about the reformative steps that they will take to improve the students' mental health.

However, in the past few years, these protests have often been used to seek the interest of a handful of individuals. During one of the cases, one of the EC members threatened me stating that he would be calling students for protests if SECC gave any verdict against him. Not bothered by his threats I still chose to convict him for his wrongdoings and no protest unfolded. However, when the institute brought in some new policy instead of peacefully discussing it with the administration, the students then started coming together to protest against the administration. Things became so nasty and out of control that the students started barging inside the administration building (Director's Office) and started creating havoc in the institute. Such callous behaviour of a handful of students not only frightened the administration but also the GSB as they had never witnessed such an irresponsible mob earlier. Moreover, these students have no sense of respect for the IITM Police and I have often seen them quarreling with them for no reason. Being the students of IIT Madras, everyone expects a level of decency from the most studious set of students in India. I am not arguing that staging a protest is a mark of indecency but what I am arguing is that staging a doctored protest is a mark of indecency.

A few years back a protest was staged in front of the IIT Madras' main gate which was a doctored protest. By doctored protest, I mean to say that the protest was funded by an individual or a set of individuals to create pressure on the IITM authority. These protesters are rewarded monetarily for maligning the reputation of the institute in front of the media houses. This way the protesters will be able to create more pressure on the institute and the institute then has to submit to their needs. In that particular protest, it was reported that students from nearby colleges were part of it because they were paid money to be part of such protests. Such types of doctored protests are not only violating the Students' Constitution but are even annihilating the spirit of democracy. In short, those who were supposed to be the custodians of the Students' Constitution (student government officials) were turning into the annihilators of the Students' Constitution by not just being part of these doctored protests but even being indifferent to such protests.

However, there have been excellent examples set by the students of IIT Madras when it came to protesting for the right cause. There have been instances when students conducted silent marches all across the institute to put forward their arguments in front of the administration. The majority of the time it is the ISBs that lead such protests educating students about current issues and expecting them to be politically aware. An educational institute like IIT Madras is a safe space where students of all ideologies are constitutionally allowed to preach their ideologies to other students and have a politically rich environment. But any form of extremism should not be accepted and tolerated by either the students or the administration because we as students are from myriad faiths, regions, languages, ethnicities, castes, sexualities, and genders, and we have to safeguard everyone's interests. This can only happen when the GSB and the students in power act responsibly as the former should not act as the puppets in the hands of the latter. And the GSB is well aware of its constitutional jurisdictions as specified in the Students' Constitution of IIT Madras.

In juxtaposition, few students among the GSB whom we refer to as backends often foul play to such an extent that ethics for them simply doesn't exist. I had heard about this foul play a lot from my seniors but was fortunate enough to experience it myself during my Chief Commissioner tenure. Yes! Fortunate enough it taught me life lessons that I believe I could not have learned later in my life and eventually made me a better version of myself. While I was busy preparing plans for Freshers' & ISS Special Election 2023, one of my core teammates from SECC (let me address her as Premika) became a pawn in the hands of one of the backends. Meenakshi being the recent entrant in my team and unaware of the foul plays, Premika reached out to Meenakshi to play the role of cupid between me and Premika. Unaware of the selfish gains Premika had, Meenakshi played the role and initiated a conversation between me and Premika on one odd night at Zaitoon in the rainy days of September. I had known Premika for at least two years before she had even become part of SECC and had always treated her as my good friend. I had a habit of sister-zoning every girl I used to meet in college because I was groomed in such an environment where it was believed that a girl and a boy could never be good friends. I used to consider Premika my sister but she was disappointed with it and asked me to only consider her as my friend.

That night when Premika expressed her feelings to me in the presence of Meenakshi. I was astonished because I never saw that coming and was never expecting Premika to propose to me in that manner. Unable to react to the situation, I denied her proposal and asked her for the rationale behind proposing to me. Premika being one of the sweetest and gorgeous girls on campus already had a boyfriend on the campus and now she was falling for me which was not easily digestible for me. In response, she expressed her feelings or at least acted to express her feelings to me by mentioning how she has been giving me hints but I was reluctant enough to catch them. After a long discussion in the middle of midnight, I finally said "I am up for it, Are you?". Premika was astonished as she was not expecting such a quick response and asked me for some time so that she could revert me with a response.

Three days had passed by and I was getting restless because I had encountered this phase of my life for the first time. That day after the team meeting got over at Ellora (sitting area next to CCD), I requested her to stay back and asked for her response. That night too it was raining heavily and Meenakshi had gone to fetch us our Swiggy order. By the time Meenakshi returned, Premika did not respond and was in a very deep thought. While we started descending from the Ellora, Premika told Meenakshi that I and Premika are going for a walk and she would return to the hostel later. As both of us were walking on the dampened roads of Adyar Avenue, Premika suddenly said "YES!". I asked "Yes, what?", and she said, "I am ready to be in a relationship with you". The moment I heard this sentence, I was so elated that I had lost my sense of mind and could not believe myself. She continued and said "But I have three conditions. First, you should not have any expectations from me. Second, we shall never hold hands with each other, roam around together in the institute, or let anyone know in the institute that we are in a relationship. Third, nothing related to our relationship should be posted on your social media account." I readily accepted all her conditions without giving a deeper thought to them, thinking that this might be a ritual that one has to perform before getting into a relationship. As a Chief Commissioner, all these conditions seemed to be in my favor as my relationship would remain concealed from the public and would invite less trouble.

My relationship officially started on 3rd September 2023 and lasted for 21 days only. Within those 21 days, we went on a trip to Pondicherry together, did multiple late-night walks, did long hours of talking and chatting, and even visited the lovers' point at Thiruvanmiyur beach. The point is that within those 21 days, Premika became the highest priority in my life, I had put my family, academics, PoR, and friends at the last rungs of my priority list. I got carried away to such an extent that one night I decided to propose to her with a watch for ₹4000 which I bought by committing the biggest mistake of my life. The mistake was that I lied to my father that I had bought a watch for my friend's friend as his bank server was down. That night, under the full moon, at the Sangam Ground I proposed to her in a very dramatic manner by kneeling on one leg and proposing her by making her wear that watch. While I gave that watch to her I said "I hope that this watch marks the beginning of a good time for both of us." Indeed the good time began for me but in the most unexpected manner.

That night, she didn't respond to my proposal the way I was expecting. Neither she was shocked nor she was sad, she was emotionless as if she receives such types of gifts every then and now. While I was heading back to the room, suddenly she said "My past boyfriend has started becoming good to me again". Unable to make sense of her statement I said "That's a good thing!". Her sentence did not make sense to me and as soon as I reached the room I started realising that I had fallen into a trap. On 24th September 2023, after defeating HS21 in the Prem Ranjan Memorial Intra-Department Cricket Tournament, I called her for a date at the Cocoa and Creme Rooftop Cafe in Adyar and spent around 3 hours with her. I was clear in my mind why I was inviting her to the cafe. On the contrary, I feel she could also sense my intent behind calling her out for a surprise date. For the initial 2.5 hours, I kept on asking her about her past boyfriend and asked her to continue her relationship with him. After getting frustrated she finally said, "I want to ride two boats at a time, so I am not leaving you as well as my past boyfriend". Hearing this I was shell-shocked and asked her "Is this your character or is the situation making you do this?". She retorted "The situation is making me do this". In response, I said, "It is better for you and your boyfriend that I should not become a bone of contention between both of you. You enjoy your life and I will enjoy mine".

That night when I was back in my room I was heartbroken and did not know what to do because the person whom I trusted the most in life turned out to be a traitor. The next morning at 5 AM I received a call from my father asking me to reach Himachal immediately as my grandfather had a cardiac arrest. Unable to take control of the situation I told my dad about my unavailability as the polling for the Freshers' and ISS Special Elections 2023 was scheduled the next day. Without giving a second thought, my dad angrily cut the call and he departed for Himachal alone. That day, I did not go out of my room, nor did I pick up anyone's call. I had received around 33 calls out of which 11 were from my commissioners, 5 were from my Election Officers and the rest were from the candidates who were contesting for various posts. By the afternoon, everyone (including Election Officers) had thought that Sushant had left the institute because he had done something highly unethical. However, I was in my room and I was silently reading a book titled *The India Way: Strategies for an Uncertain World* written by Dr. S. Jaishankar when I realised that one person cannot annihilate who I am.

That evening I made a surprise entry to the Election Coordinators' meeting as well as tested the portal for the polling that was scheduled the next day. At the portal testing, the Chief Election Officer Prof. Anbarasu looked at me and said "Sushant learn to stay strong and if there is any help you need, we all are always there for you". By the time I reached my room, I was so done with Premika that her presence in my team was bothering me a lot. I was so fed up with her that I submitted my resignation letter one night before polling day to Prof. Anup Kumar Bhandari (SECC Faculty Advisor) from the post of SECC Chief Commissioner stating personal reasons. Resigning from SECC means resigning from SEC but because the polling was scheduled the next day, I didn't want to bring a bad name to the SEC. So I decided that I would resign from SECC today and once the polling was over I will resign from SEC later. On the day of polling even though I was working along with Premika the whole day, I conducted the polling day successfully by having a clown face.

The next day, Prof. Anup called me for a personal meeting regarding my resignation. By then my father had informed me that my grandfather was doing good and everything was fine at home. Feeling at ease a bit, I went to meet the Professor and took back my resignation stating that everything now is under control. Glad about my decision, Prof. Anup wished me the best of luck and asked me to focus more on academics.

Once the elections got over there was a void in my life, a void where there was no Premika, no SEC, and no friends. I got so stressed out of this void that I became a workaholic and was making my team do more work than they could practically do. Still unsatisfied with myself, I started smoking and drinking in an uncontrollable manner which not only deteriorated my health but even amplified the void. Finally one day, Meenakshi had a conversation with me about my relationship with Premika and told me what she was really afraid of telling me. Till then I always used to think that Meenakshi was the reason for my falling into the 'love trap' but that day I realised that she was being used as bait to make me fall into this 'love trap'. No one in the institute other than Meenakshi asked me to stop drinking-smoking and focus on my academics when I was down in the dumps. Seeing a ray of hope, I gradually rebuilt myself under the firm guidance of Meenakshi who now was no more like a friend to me but was more like a real sister to me.

With time I learned to keep my personal and professional life separate and realised that it was a well-planned trap that was executed to bring fissures in the team by one of the backends. However, with God's grace and Meenakshi's smartness, the team not only remained united but was appreciated by everyone for conducting the ISS Special Elections so efficiently. With this, I got to experience the sacrifices that an SECC Commissioner is expected to make while the other student government officials don't have to even bother about it. As SEC Commissioners we cannot rely on anyone else other than our fellow Commissioners who are always partners in crime together. At the time of Elections, backends become so active and brutal that they give threat calls to the Commissioners' friends (boyfriend or girlfriend) and sometimes even to the Commissioners' parents. I recall an incident when my mother got a scam call stating that I have been convicted for a rape case at the Kotturpuram Police Station. She received this scam call at the same time when the Freshers' and ISS Special Elections 2023 were going on. In my case, because I didn't have any close friend or girlfriend to whom they could bother, the backend decided to bother my parents which was no less than a nightmare for them.

No other EC or SLC member has to go through so much mental harassment that an SEC Commissioner has to go through. Before falling into such a love trap, I only used to hear it from my senior commissioners but after the incident, I realised that being an SECC Commissioner is more difficult than being any other student government official at IIT Madras. The compromises and the negotiations that an SECC Commissioner had to do at a personal level were beyond any sort of compensation that the institute could ever provide except self-satisfaction. Before 2023 there only used to be 1 or 2 applicants for the post of SECC Commissioner because of the tough commitments but today the applicants' number has increased to 7 or 8. All this has happened because of the consistent efforts of the past SECC Commissioners who have not just ameliorated the commitments with time but have even widened the potentiality of the position of the SECC Commissioner. During my tenure, I even created a WA group called SECC Inner Circle where all SECC Commissioners can give their suggestions or opinions to the current commissioners as and when required because some time or another we all were partners in the same crime.

As we all were preparing for SGE 2024, the backends too were devising ingenious methods of disrupting the smooth functioning of SEC so that SGE 2024 can be rigged easily.

Being aware of the deceptive politics of the EC members I got the polling week added to the even semester timetable after a thorough consultation with the EC members through the Time Table Committee. Unlike SGE 2023, if Quiz 1 gets postponed then the polling day too can be easily postponed. The rationale behind adding polling week and not polling day in the timetable was that any one day within the polling week could be the polling day. The polling day shall be fixed after the election schedule is released by the SEC, thereby safeguarding the autonomy of the SEC. Simultaneously, I conducted consultations with the GSB members, EC members, and faculty regarding the changes that they wish to bring to the Election Manual of SGE 2024.

Moreover, most of the students think that when the SEC is active, the SECC vanishes, and when the SECC is active the SEC vanishes. As per the Rules of Procedure of SECC, at the time of elections, SECC's business shall be headed by at least one of the commissioners.[9] This is exactly what we did during the SGE 2024 when we received 6 more complaints. Over and above the cases, I also curated an Ethical Code Draft Committee that was headed by Mr. Karthik Kurimindla who was an SECC Coordinator in SECC 2023-24 but is currently an SECC Commissioner in SECC 2024-25. The objective of the committee was to create a student-friendly IITM Honour Code or Student Ethics Code that inculcates moral values among the students over some time. This was a first-of-its-kind initiative taken by SECC which involved members from GSB, the Wellness Centre (Dr. Jinna Bordoloi), and the administration. The Committee submitted its draft to the DoST and is expecting it to be launched in the upcoming academic section as an IITM Students' Ethics Code which they would sign in the presence of their parents at the time of admission.

Since India too was going through the 18th General Elections, the impact of SGE 2024 was magnified and the responsibility over the shoulders of the SEC increased multifold. The Director's Office called the three SEC Commissioners to make the institute elections one of its kind by conducting full-scale blockchain-based polling for the first time in India. The Director Prof. V. Kamakoti, agreed to grant us a fund of ₹2 lakhs for developing a blockchain-based voting portal for SGE 2024. Since 2021, IIT Madras has been known for advancements in the Electoral Process and has collaborated with the Election Commission of India (ECI) as well to build a blockchain-based voting system.[10] SEC being the harbinger of electoral technological advancement, had deployed a blockchain-based voting system first time in the SLC Speaker's Elections in 2022. Later it was deployed for SGE 2023 during Ardra's tenure which faced some glitches but finally, it was deployed at a full-fledged scale in SGE 2024 under my tenure.[11]

In this journey of SGE 2024, our new mentor was Mr. Ruthramoorthy Senthamaraikannan (Liaison Officer at IIT Madras) with whom we commissioners had planned to launch a campaign and encourage students to vote not only in SGE 2024 but even in General Elections 2024. For SEC the prime motive behind having electoral reforms is to increase the voter turnout of SGEs. Being the premiere institute of India the voter turnout in the past SGEs has not been so encouraging, as per official records the past voter turnouts are as follows: SGE 2020 - 47.15%, SGE 2021 - 45.33%, SGE 2022 - 40%,

SGE 2023 - 48.67%. I firmly believe that SGE is the biggest festival of IIT Madras which is celebrated by every student at a time when the semester is at its peak. Moreover, I believe that conducting and participating in Saarang (cultural fest of IITM), Shaastra (technical fest of IITM), or any event of IIT Madras is much easier than SGE. SGE is a one-month-long event that is not just a humongous challenge for SEC but even for the students to actively participate in it. A mass event happening around the quizzes of a semester not only discourages SEC members but even distracts GSB from their academics for at least 2 months. However, without fail, SEC has been conducting SGEs for the past several years even though the commission has to start planning for it 2 months ahead of the event.

Keeping the shortcomings of the past SGEs in mind, we launched a campaign called *Operation 100: Every Vote Matters* to channel our efforts in a streamlined manner to achieve high voter turnout in SGE 2024. We conducted Briefing Hour Sessions to sensitise students about the campaign, conducted cultural dance and folk music events, introduced E-Kart Polling Booths, curated a wall painting near the CCW office, introduced an online competition called Meme-ing Democracy, and recruited 100+ campaigning ambassadors. One of the most challenging things of SGE 2024 was to conduct Soapbox for the EC positions as the AAS soapbox in 2023 saw a scuffle which we were adamant to not repeat. The soapbox alone had a budget of ₹5 lakhs and was planned in such a manner that from the administration to the students, everyone appreciated us for conducting soapboxes so peacefully. We had barricaded the whole SAC, had put a cap on the strength of the audience, had set up projectors and speakers, had registered the audience using their Insitute IDs, and had even increased the IITM security. SECC conducted its only Voices of the State lecture for the year 2024 by inviting Dr. V. Palanikumar, the Election Commissioner of State Election Commission of Tamil Nadu for an inaugural lecture at IIT Madras.[12]

Unlike past SGEs, for SGE 2024, my commission emphasised the Social Media Policy that was enforced by the DoST Office to reduce cyberbullying during campus elections. With the introduction of the Social Media Policy, cyberbullying decreased to a significant extent and more female candidates were seen participating in SGE 2024, especially for the positions of EC. However, there were a couple of instances that were brought under control to ameliorate the impact of corruption at the earliest. At the time of campaigning, I received a mail in my mailbox stating that one of the SEC members was altering the manifestos and feasibility reports of the candidates. On digging deep, I found out that Premika was the one who had been changing the submitted documents of the selected candidates for her gains. After some time, she surrendered to me stating that she knew she had performed a corrupt practice but was not aware of the reason behind doing this. From my detailed investigation within 12 hours, I got to know that she was being asked by her friend to upload the new manifesto for a candidate who was contesting for the post of HSS Department Research Legislator. Once the student had won the election, he would have voted for Premika's past boyfriend to the post of SLC Speaker because only the legislators vote for the post of SLC Speaker. On realising this fact, I convened an emergency meeting with my commissioners and Election Officers (Chief

Election Officer - Prof. Sudakar Chandran & Deputy Election Officer - Prof. M. Jeganmohan) and canceled the candidature of the student whose manifesto was being altered. However, Premika was so distressed by the SEC's decision that she wanted to resign from her post as a candidate and had to lose his candidature because of her corrupt act. At that particular point, Premika was adamant in filing her resignation which I vehemently criticised stating that the backend shall use her resignation as a reason for re-conducting SGE 2024 on the grounds of SEC's mismanagement.

Annoyed by the foolish act of Premika, I was very angry with her both at a personal and professional level because now I was sure that she was an intruder in our team who had been more loyal to one of the backends than the SEC. The next day, Premika apologised to the SECC Commissioners in front of the Election Officers and assured us that she wouldn't repeat the same. Unable to trust her totally, the Election Officers cautioned me that she should not ascend the ladder of the PoR hierarchy within SECC at any cost. After a few hours of normalcy, we received two more emails outrightly accusing Premika of being involved in corrupt practices of altering the documents of the candidates contesting for the post of legislators. To deal with such critical complaints, I took the permission of the Election Officers to keep Premika out of the investigation and transferred the case to SECC as the SEC does not have any constitutional power to deal with the unethical acts executed by the GSB members even at the time of elections. We investigated that at least 10 candidates were contesting for the post of legislator from various departments and hostels who had used the official account of one of the EC members to draft their similar manifestos and feasibility reports. It was the same EC member whom I had suspended earlier during my tenure. Unaware of what was happening under his nose, he was cautioned about this corrupt act and so were the other EC members. The Heads of one of the SGAOs under that EC member had a nexus among themselves which Premika was also part of, the objective of the Nexus was to look for naive candidates who were desperate for assistance. Making use of their desperation, the Nexus copied the detailed manifesto and feasibility report by the deception of a junior who was also contesting for the hostel legislator position. Irrespective of the department or hostel post, all the candidates had the same manifesto and feasibility report because they were contesting for the post of legislator.

But the real issue was the usage of the official Canva account (a graphic designing tool) of one of the EC members for which GSB pays for its yearly subscription was being used to make election documents for a handful of the candidates and the candidates were unaware about it. After a detailed investigation, we SEC Commissioners concluded that the candidates should have 48 hours of campaigning restriction while the Nexus should be interrogated by SECC.

At the time of SECC's investigation, the members of the Nexus accepted their mistakes and we suspended them from their PoRs till the end of their tenure. Whenever a suspension or a dismissal sanction used to be imposed, I used to publicly send that email so that the GSB who have given legitimacy to these PoR holders to lead them in various spheres should be aware of the wrongdoings that their PoR holders have done. Within 24 hours, SECC received a mail from the Deputy

Registrar (Students) stating that owing to the deteriorating mental health of the accused PoR holders, the decision of SECC has been revoked. I was not upset about it because I had publicly imposed my sanctions over these PoR holders while the Deputy Registrar (Students) had sent a direct mail to the SEC. The GSB had received the message that it was supposed to receive and surprisingly Premika retorted over us for not making her part of the investigation, even though I had personally informed her about her abstinence from the investigation in consultation with the Chief Election Officer.

Envious of me, the Nexus decided to file a false case over me for mismanaging the institute resources, recruiting coordinators based on favoritism, and imposing a false charge over me of molesting a girl during the interrogation. To resolve their complaint, the DoST constituted an ad-hoc committee under the Chairmanship of former SEC Faculty Advisor Prof. Ratna Kumar whose responsibility was to deal with my case and check the constitutionality of SECC's decision regarding the Nexus. From the initial itself, the Committee seemed to be biased against SEC as they were failing to find even a single flaw against us. Out of frustration, they made my Heads of Secretariats write an apology letter for mistakenly opening their assignments using the official email ID of the SECC Secretariat which is in no comparison to the unethical acts that were performed by the Nexus. Finally, the ad-hoc committee concluded that I had not mismanaged any resources, did not propagate any kind of favoritism, and did not molest any girl during the interrogation (as Meenakshi too was in the same interrogation room who became my witness). However, they chose to revoke SECC's decision on the grounds of being too harsh on the students.

In my belief, what exactly would have happened was that at the time of the manifesto manipulation, Premika did it intentionally on the demand of the Nexus as all the Nexus members were her classmates and close friends. At the time of Premika's conviction the way Nexus compromised itself by not disclosing her identity, in return when Nexus was convicted they wanted Premika's assistance during their investigation in ameliorating the sanctions imposed by SECC. But since the latter did not happen, Premika became annoyed with SECC Commissioners and chose to disobey by being indifferent to all the formal orders of SECC. Premika was no longer acting like one of us as she chose to take sick leaves during the time of releasing the Final Nomination List due to which Meenakshi had to burn her midnight oil even though she was sick too. On one side Premika decided to have a good time with her friends on the other hand we SECC members had to work day and night to make the SGE 2024 a grand success. I still recall the days, when Meenakshi used to explode with her frustration over me but was sincere enough to get the work done.

I didn't formally disclose Premika's relationship with Nexus because at that time the elections were at stake and maintaining GSB's trust in SEC was my utmost priority. Moreover, the main objective of the Nexus was to make their friend win the SLC Speaker election for which they needed votes from the legislators. Since the legislators were convicted by the SEC for using institute funds and official Canva accounts, 8 out of 10 legislators lost the elections while only 1 legislator won the elections. I always believed that GSB is the supreme power in our student government but for the first time in my life, I witnessed it with my open eyes.

It was the same time when one of my coordinators Mr. Kaushik Raja had to face a very unfortunate incident. His father had met an accident a few days back and he had gone to the hospital to meet him. But sadly, due to medical negligence, his father passed away in the hospital. I being the Chief Commissioner of a team whose member was going through the worst part of his life decided to meet Kaushik in his hometown on the same day when his father passed away. I went to Cuddalore to give Kuashik moral support and the moment he saw me he felt light-hearted and motivated. I assured him all sorts of support as a senior that I could give him and asked him to take his time to settle first and not bother about PoR.

Simultaneously, keeping the PoR conundrum in mind, I opined the idea of framing a *PoR Charter* that would be a one-stop solution for all GSB members to refer to the recruitment process of various PoRs and seek redressal if any team or individual is not abiding by the same. The 99-page PoR Charter drew its power from the Rulebooks and is subject to change as and when the Rulebooks undergo changes. The charter was not only circulated among the GSB but was even circulated among the Faculty Advisors to genuinely know their roles at the time of team selection. Meenakshi being the former Editor in T5E knew how to edit documents in a manner that could be easily interpreted by eveyrone. The same magic she showed in the drafting of the PoR Charter as well which I believe is one of the most sorted documents of the SECC published to date.

Like always, one of the EC members unhappy with SEC's progress decided to disrupt it by convincing the Director that the turnout would be low due to a lack of contestants for the various positions of Executive Council. Taking the suggestion of the EC member seriously, the Director convened a meeting with SEC Commissioners, DoST, and the Election Officers. In the meeting, the Director said that he wants the nomination portal to be reopened. After a bit of agitation from Tejaswini, I finally accepted the Director's proposal on the condition that we would be mentioning in our mail that the nomination portal has been reopened as per the Director's instruction.[13] To which Director agreed but didn't realise that meddling with SEC's autonomy not only shuns the efforts of a team but even exploits the patience of the GSB who are improperly represented by a few of the EC members. We released the mail and the GSB was not satisfied with the Director's decision as they felt that SEC was becoming a puppet in the hands of the Director.

To a certain extent, this was true but the real culprit was that particular EC member who didn't want a married female mother pursuing a PhD (Ms. Robin Rathi currently the Research Affairs Secretary) to contest for an EC position unanimously. To decrease her winning chances, the nomination portal was reopened to allow another candidate to contest for the same position that was unapologetically endorsed by the same EC member. As per the Election Manual, EC members cannot endorse candidates during elections. However, in this particular case, we did not have any evidence that could prove that the EC member was endorsing the candidate in SGE 2024.

For the first time in the history of SGEs, the SEC reopened the nomination portal only for 24 hours. We had indeed received more nominations than before but it came at the cost of meddling with SEC's autonomy and integrity. However, a rumor spread across the institute that the Director didn't want to have a mother with an infant win an EC position in the institute which is absolutely false. The mistake that the Director committed was to blindly believe the EC member which led to the tarnishing of his reputation after this particular incident.

But little did we know that the Director was going to again meddle with us when one of the candidates (for an EC position) did not submit his election documents on time. Unable to submit election documents on time, the nomination of the candidate was canceled and the candidate portrayed it as a technical glitch. Within one hour a meeting was convened in the DoST Office where a handful of EC members in power questioned me and Meenakshi about the cancelation of the nomination. The EC members were so frustrated with the SEC that they accused us of being the most student-unfriendly organisation and asked me and my commissioners to resign from our posts. The HAS was so frustrated with me that he asked DoST "Sir, how can we bypass Sushant's decision?". On the other hand, the Cultural Affairs Secretary started yelling in the room "We EC members should be allowed to conduct elections and should not depend on Sushant's inefficient commission". In retaliation, I said, "Then there won't be any difference between the IITM SGE and the Pakistan General Elections."

The candidate became so hopeless that the EC members had to again reach out to the Director to make us accept his nomination. Again, we sent a similar mail and allowed the students to submit their documents within the next 12 hours. The supporters of the opposing candidate for the same EC position were annoyed with the Director and decided to protest against the Director by writing public emails. As the situation was becoming worse, the Director finally said "I am not going to get involved in this and I never forced SEC to take any decision. Whatsoever decision SEC takes shall be considered as the final decision".

Once I got this confirmation from the Director, I was sure that never is the Director going to blindly believe in the EC members from now on. After this, the polling went on smoothly and the SGE 2024 registered the highest voting turnout of 59.43% for the very first time in the history of IIT Madras. In fact, after a long time, the voting turnout crossed the 50% mark and was indeed a remarkable achievement for the SEC. Then came the time of appreciation which we broadly earned because of the collaborative approach of SEC with all the teams in the institute that made SGE 2024 a grand success. A documentary of the whole *Operation 100 & SGE 2024* has been made by IITM TV which I would suggest you all watch to get a better understanding of elections at IIT Madras.[14]

Though the SGE 2024 was over the elections for the post of SLC Speaker were still left to be done. As per the Election Manual, the polling for the SLC Speaker Election should happen within 2 weeks immediately from the date of announcing the SGE 2024 results. By this time I was so sick that I had almost lost 10 kg weight in 2 months and had consistent abdominal pain. On being investigated by the doctor, I was asked to leave for home on an emergency basis as I had symptoms of TB. To conduct the polling at the earliest and without any hassle I devised the plan for the SLC Speaker Elections with a new twist. On the advice of Meenakshi, I agreed to conduct the polling on the same day just after the soapbox was completed. I left for my home one day before the polling day and made Meenakshi the ad-hoc SEC Chief Commissioner to oversee the SLC Speaker soapbox and polling. Like always, without any failure Meenakshi did a fabulous job and proved herself to be one of the finest commissioners SEC had seen so far.

Finally, SGE 2024 came to an end and a new phase of SECC was going to be unleashed. I made the required changes to the SECC Rules of Procedure by adding definitions of the Latin terms in the document and other modifications so that GSB could easily comprehend the document. We commissioners also proposed a set of Constitutional Amendments after a thorough consultation with bodies like Vannam (IIT Madras' student body for the welfare of LGBTQ+), MITR, and so on. After completing all my major responsibilities I chose to dig up the past and do something that no SECC Commissioner would have done to date. I filed a complaint against Premika for performing an act of corruption by manipulating manifestos at the time of SGE 2024. The rationale behind launching this complaint was to set an example in the commission for future commissioners to be aware of their responsibilities more than their selfish gains. The IDCS denied taking such type of complaint and requested DoST to form an ad-hoc committee to deal with this complaint. In an ad-hoc committee under the Chairmanship of Former Election Commissioner Prof. V.

Sriram, all SECC Commissioners including Premika were interrogated for hours.

My journey in SECC began with a disciplinary committee and reached its fag end again by a disciplinary committee where I was sitting on the other side of the table like the first time. Life is like a cycle and so was my tenure at SECC, I reached the same point from where I started my journey. The Committee never declared its decision nor did I bother to check on it. Meenakshi became the new Chief Commissioner of SECC, and Karthik and Kaushik became her co-commissioners. Later during the semester, DoST invited us for lunch at the same spot where I learned the most brutal lessons of my life and I believe you know the spot about which I am talking about.

Chapter 5

Marching Towards Protopia (2024 Onwards)

The revolutionary approach of mine though helped SECC & SEC to achieve 3Ts but could not bring solutions to all the problems of the student politics at IITM. This is because I was striving for extremes which is never rewarding to anyone as is the golden mean as rightly pointed out by Aristotle. Drawing on the same lines, protopia is a golden mean that is in between dystopia and utopia which can be achieved only by gradual progress over time. This progress has to happen not just within SECC & SEC but has to happen at all levels of student government at IIT Madras beginning with student government officials and ending with GSB.

The primary issue with the current IITM student politics is that the vision the drafters of the Students' Constitution had for student politics has not materialised as intended. Instead, it has taken up the ugly shape of the *kurtaclad* politics which is impeding the progress of the student politics from achieving protopia. The very idea of constituting a unicameral legislature with the absence of the opposition, prohibition on the formation of political parties, the creation of a quasi-judicial body - SECC, and many more initiatives were taken to make IITM a safe space for students to explore various political ideologies for the greater good of the campus. The reason behind having such a unique student government structure at IITM is to encourage students to discover the best of political practices and achieve a protopia that sets an example for other democracies to be inspired by. On the contrary, the IITM student government is becoming similar to the traditional democracies due to which the issues which are faced by traditional democracies are being faced by the IITM student government as well. I am not arguing that traditional democracies are inefficient but what I am arguing is that the modern government structure that was devised for IITM is not meeting its objective of creating a *sui generis* political environment. An environment that suits the habitat of the bright minds of the world where politics meet a new definition of technology and practicality.

Here is a simple way to understand, the center of attraction for contesting in elections is not for serving the GSB and gaining satisfaction but to unlock its job prospects in the future. As I had mentioned before to achieve a high-paying job all you need is a PoR peak/International exposure/National-level achievement along with the required skill set. However, in the past few years, a new trend has emerged where becoming an EC member can unlock one's chances of getting a decent job. This trend gradually annihilated the idea of selfless service as every candidate used to contest for the EC post to have better career opportunities rather than serving the GSB for the betterment of IIT Madras. Empirically this can be proven if we look at the general trend of the CGPAs of the candidates who are contesting for EC posts. In the SGE 2022, only two candidates had a CGPA of approximately 9. In SGE 2023, this number dropped to just one candidate, and by SGE 2024, not a single candidate had a CGPA of around 9. This trend is also common to see among other elected positions as well like Department and Hostel positions. I am not trying to prove any correlation here between a high CGPA and better political performance but what I am arguing is that earlier students of high academic vigor used to contest for the posts of EC to set an example for the institute and the students. Now EC members are no longer acting as the role models of the institute instead they are becoming mongers of dirty politics where knowledge is downsised by propaganda.

I believe in a simple logic, students with 9 and above CG have fulfilled their academic commitments and have enough time to devote themselves to the service of the GSB. To substantiate my statement let me give you my example, I joined the team when I had a CG of 9.29 (until 2nd semester), ascended to the position of Commissioner with a CG of 9.54 (until 4th semester), and finally retired from the position of Chief Commissioner with a CG of 9.44 (until 8th semester). Students with such high academic commitments often do not indulge in dirty politics as they have a constraint of time and are more efficient in getting things done quickly. On the other hand, students with a CGPA below 8 are often carefree about their academics and choose to be more politically agile than what is required. Such students not only act as impediments in the smooth functioning of student politics but even turn out to be less efficient. I propagate all these arguments because I have seen the trend closely by being part of the student government for the past three years. There is no doubt that there are always exceptions to the aforementioned trend but to have a public-spirited intent it is important to have the scenarios under which such intent can be generated.

Let me give you all one more example here, the current RAS of IITM, Ms. Robin Rathi (2024-25) has more commitments than what an ordinary IITM student would have because she is not pursuing only PhD but is also a married woman with a 2-year-old infant.[15] Over-the-top contesting for the post of RAS without taking the help of any backend is only possible when one has a clean and clear intent. From an academic point of view, I would argue that Ms. Robin had cleared her Compri (Comprehensive Exam) well before the mandated time thereby beginning her research well ahead of the stipulated time which allowed her to even think of contesting for the post of RAS. Usually, PhD scholars appear for Compri after 2 years of joining the institute and often struggle to clear the exam as it marks the official beginning of their PhD research. After personally knowing Ms. Robin, in my opinion, she is one of the finest RAS that the institute has ever seen as she has set an example for other students especially other EC members who often look for excuses to escape challenges rather than facing them with a smile.

If top-notch positions like SECC, EC, and SLC are taken over by students like Ms. Robin then the student government structure of IITM can go through a paradigm shift. A shift where IITM is producing politically awakened and morally upright students who make informed choices keeping everyone's interests in mind. One of the living examples that student government officials of IIT Madras should get inspired from is IIT Delhi. The Student Affairs Council (SAC) of IIT Delhi is the student government of IIT Delhi that is highly active in its endeavors and way ahead of its time.

The SAC of IIT Delhi has a well-dedicated webpage that mentions the completed, ongoing, and upcoming tasks of SAC in an organised manner. They don't just have a repository of records of their legislative council but have records of all the constitutional bodies.[16] Further, they have three unique executive positions that most of the IITs do not have - the position of married research scholar representative, differently abled representative, and day scholar representative. The presence of such diverse secretaries leads to the creation of holistic representation which not only motivates GSB to actively participate in student politics but even encourages them to guide the student politics in the right direction. During my Chief Commissioner tenure, I proposed a constitutional amendment to introduce an EC position called Secretary for Students with Disability (SSwD) which has not been actualised to date. The reason behind such a lethargic response is the lack of awareness among the student government officials towards their past officials and their contributions. Instead of building a robust infrastructure on the strong foundation laid by their seniors (for example deployment of the blockchain-based voting portal), every student government official tries to build a new foundation which not only wastes precious time of their limited tenure but often leads to negligible progress. To make significant progress in student politics, officials often have to put in more effort than expected, often at the expense of their personal commitments. When I joined SECC, I weighed 81 kg, and by the time I left, I weighed 62 kg. Hence, if someone is interested in losing weight then you all must join SECC without any second thought.

In the following paragraphs, I am going to mention the areas of improvement in the student government structure of IIT Madras which I believe can also be incorporated by other institutes to refine their student politics for the greater good of their student community.

IIT Madras Honour Code/Students' Ethics Code should be adopted and enforced by the IITM at the earliest for students to become morally upright and socially responsible for every action that they perform within the precincts of the institute. Unlike any other change, social change is the only change that takes the longest amount of time to get enforced because it can never be imposed it can always be adopted. Therefore, the day students are admitted to IITM, in the presence of their parents or guardians, the students should acknowledge the IITM Honour Code. During my Chief Commissioner tenure, I had constituted this Students' Ethics Code Committee which comprised people from various fields to make a Code that allows students to flourish ethically. The Code included the attributes of mental health as well which makes it different from any other formal document of IITM that has been drafted so far. As per our Students' Constitution, IITM had a Students' Honour Code until 2019, but with the advent of the pandemic, the administration did not reinstate the Honour Code. Renowned institutes like Harvard already have a full-fledged Students' Honour Code which prescribes the conduct of the students.[17]

Directive Principle of Campus Policy (DPCP) is the new section that should be added to the Students' Constitution or should be separately proposed as a new bill in the SLC. The bill should take adaptations from the Directive Principles of State Policy which is part of the Constitution of India. The objective behind introducing DPCP is to set goals for the directionless IITM student government to function in a guided fashion. Rather than framing and executing laws on an ad-hoc basis, the IITM student government should follow the DPCP for the greater good of the student community. Based on DPCP, the student government every one year can formulate a plan that should be abided by the student government officials during their tenure. I have noticed that almost every candidate during the SGE presents a similar kind of manifesto that draws its existence from past incomplete manifestos. Therefore, the plan should be flexible enough for the newly elected government officials to not just introduce new ideas but to even achieve the greater goals of DPCP by using unique methods.

Mandatory Leadership Training Program for Candidates should be conducted before elections and should be made mandatory for all the candidates who are planning to contest for Students' General Elections. These sessions will cover areas such as decision-making, conflict resolution, ethical governance, and communication skills. The goal is to ensure that candidates understand the responsibilities associated with their roles and are equipped to serve effectively irrespective of the election results. This reform will help transition elections from popularity contests to merit-driven selections of capable leaders. In general such programs shall also lead to personality development among the students irrespective of their interests in contesting for SGE or not. A more detailed set of workshops and orientation sessions including OBT (Outbounding Training) should be organised for the newly elected and nominated student government officials. These workshops should also serve as a bridge between outgoing student government officials and newly recruited ones, facilitating the seamless transfer of knowledge.

Fastracking Constitutional Amendments is the need of the hour for the changing IITM to adapt to the changing needs of the students. Constitutional amendments have been one of the most painstaking tasks in the student governance of IITM which is gradually becoming an impediment to the progress of student politics. During my tenure, I had proposed the introduction of an SSwD as the new EC position which has to date not been discussed either in BoS or in the Senate. Thereby denying the right of equal opportunity to students with disability who are taking admission at IIT Madras in large numbers due to its conducive environment. In most of the cases, I have seen that the SLC Speakers do not bother about the status of the past constitutional amendments which had been sent to either BoS or Senate for its further approval.

Periodic Legislations are expected to happen for the healthy functioning of the GSB rather than simply passing budgets and resolutions which are simply temporary. The most recent bill that was passed in SLC was in the year 2019 and it was regarding the 'No Tobacco Policy'. After the pandemic, I have not seen even a single bill getting passed in the SLC or addressing the issues of the GSB in the form of legislation. On the contrary, SLC has started acting like an executive branch where it overlooks the proper implementation of the laws rather than framing the laws. I do agree that the three branches of democracy are not water-tight containers and share a significant amount of common ground. But that doesn't mean that each branch can compromise on its core responsibilities. Therefore, the SLC legislators should be more particular about introducing bills by taking the help of the SLC Speaker's SGAOs rather than performing subsidiary responsibilities. The SLC Speaker can have designated periods of the year (like Winter Session and Monsoon Session) where bills can be given prime focus and can be enforced for the greater good of the campus. Rather than giving their legislative powers to the administration (primarily DoST), the SLC should ponder upon the prevalent issues on the campus and formulate laws on the same. The bills should follow the existing laws of India, the laws of Tamil Nadu, the laws of Chennai, and the laws that are formulated by the IITM administration to be an all-encompassing document.

The Post-Election Accountability Mechanism has to be made vibrant enough to ensure the supremacy of the GSB in IITM student politics. Once elected, representatives must present a once-in-two-month progress report detailing their work on manifesto promises as mentioned in the Students' Constitution. These reports should be publicly available and be followed by a Townhall meeting where students can question, provide feedback, and suggest further improvements. Such transparency ensures that secretaries remain committed to their campaign promises and maintain accountability to the GSB. This should also happen at the hostel and department level where each hostel or department general body meeting should review the progress of their legislators.

Sensitizing the Students about the evils of student politics and giving them a neutral view of student politics would cease the transfer of political malpractices among the students. Having a formal channel for discussing student politics rather than informally getting to know about the same would be a desirable option. A 5-minute introduction during the orientation of the freshers would not solve the purpose. In the presence of their parents/guardians, there should be a detailed orientation session of at least 15 minutes about the student political scenario of the campus so that the students adapt to the political culture and do not become victims of either identity or deceptive politics. One should understand that as an institute we should not be ashamed of the system which we have created for our welfare. Talking and discussing politics will not only make students aware of the current happenings but will even motivate them to contribute to the political structure of the institute by responsibly participating in it. Treating student politics as a social taboo will just make the GSB puppets in the hands of either the administration or the student government officials, thereby stripping them of their constitutional supremacy.

Awaken the Voter is often considered to be the sole responsibility of the Student Election Commission but is often the mark of a failed government structure. In simple words, if the voters of a given government structure choose not to cast their votes then that means the voters have either lost interest or faith in the government structure itself. If we look at the voter turnout for the past 5 years of IIT Madras, one can notice that only once did the turnout cross the 50% mark. This refers to the fact that half of the GSB believes that their vote doesn't possess any value in the political structure of IIT Madras. The non-voting students believe that irrespective of their votes, every year there would be the same type of student government officials who won't be doing anything for them. Otherwise, all it takes is 15-20 minutes to cast a vote that half of the student population believes has no value. It is quintessential for a healthy democracy that the GSB participates in SGEs with full enthusiasm thereby making the students realise the value of their votes. On the contrary, the only benefit of having backends in the institute is to encourage students to cast votes during the elections which still doesn't justify the unethical acts executed by them.

Mandatory 15 Days Off Policy for all student government officials should be there where the members of the SLC, EC, and SECC are statutorily obliged to take 15 days off from their responsibilities. One of the reasons for having high mental and physical health issues among student government officials is the consistent work pressure that they all carry from the day they take up the responsibilities. Being a student government official should not be torture for the individual but should be a duty that mutually benefits both the GSB as well as the individual. By introducing such a policy, the productivity of the student government officials will increase multifold and would be a much-needed break from the hectic schedule of an official. The policy can be designed in such a manner that specified months of the tenure of different officials should be designated as holidays. It would not be practical to assign the same month for all the officials and hence it should be left to the whims of the officials to decide on their own. However, I strongly believe that SECC Commissioners should at least frame this policy for themselves as they are working 24x7, and even during vacations which is highly exploitative on their part.

A Delegated Legislature is something that I believe shall speed up the process of formulating laws and policies in IITM to address the issues which often not are directly dealt with by SLC. In the case of IITM, I argue that the SECC should be given the authority to frame delegated legislature on issues that do not create much relevance for SLC to deal with. For instance, the introduction of the PoR Charter is enforceable only because it draws its power from the EC members' Rulebooks. To create by-laws related to the PoR Charter, SECC currently does not have any power to achieve the same. Therefore, SECC should be granted the right to frame and enforce a delegated legislature that would not only bring law enforcement at the grassroots but would also allow nominated members to exercise this power at the testing times.

De-ratification is the Need of the Hour at a time when firing students from their respective PoRs has become more common because of the undisputed powers granted to the EC members. As mentioned before, ratification refers to the public legitimacy that the individuals receive from the representatives of the GSB to officially start their PoR journey. However, at the time of firing the same set of individuals, the SLC plays no role which is unfair on the part of the individuals. Ideally, the process of de-ratification should be conducted where the same set of people who had ratified the individual should vote for her removal if they feel the evidence submitted by the EC member is valid. I do agree that this process is no different from the impeachment process, however, a simple majority in the SLC shall confirm the de-ratification of the individual. At the time of de-ratification, the individual shall also be given the chance to present her case in front of the august presence of the SLC legislators.

Reforms in the SGE are desirable but should be enforced keeping the interest of GSB in mind. One of the most urgent reforms that should be taken up by the SEC is to conduct special elections for the vacant posts. As per the Election Manual, once the elections are done, the vacant posts shall be filled by the admin as per the due process. However, on having vacant positions again, the SEC should conduct Special Elections as mentioned in the Students' Constitution. To date, other than SECC 2023-24 no other commission has conducted Special Elections due to lack of awareness about the same.

As per the 2006 J.M. Lyngdoh (former Chief Election Commissioner of India) Committee Report, the SEC should frame laws related to the expenditure that the candidates have incurred during the elections. Such financial accountability will not only make candidates financially responsible but would even help them earn the respect of GSB which they all eagerly look forward to. As per the report, the maximum permitted expenditure per candidate should be ₹5000. Once the results are declared, each candidate should share their financial statements with the SEC and the SEC should publish the audited accounts on its website. In the case of the non-compliance, the candidature of the candidate should be nullified.[18] Moreover, I strongly consider the addition of an eligibility criteria in the Election Manual for the candidates which specify that the students running for various positions should clear all their pending fees. If they are unable to do so due to some inevitable reasons then they should get an exemption from the DoST in the case of academic fees and the CCW Chairman in the case of hostel/mess fees. I propose such a stringent clause keeping in mind the deteriorating financial health of the institute which I believe has to be addressed with utmost sincerity by everyone including the GSB. This clause in no manner violates the right to equal opportunity but is setting a standard for the candidates to fulfill before contesting for the elections of the premier institute of India.

Revival of FAC is required to instill the value of fiscal discipline across the student government of IIT Madras. In multiple cases, I have seen actual expenditure going beyond the proposed expenditure for which no accountability is taken by the student government officials. As mentioned before there have been multiple incidents of financial misappropriation within the student government structure and they still exist as no formal body is keeping a check on the same. Therefore, constituting FAC should not be at the helm of the SLC Speaker but should be independent of it so that the SLC Speaker cannot regulate the FAC as per her whims. Every year around ₹2 crore is allocated to the IITM student government from the Gymkhana Funds to conduct student welfare activities throughout the year. However, other than the proposed budget in the SLC, no auditing happens of the actual expenditure that is incurred by the officials after their tenure is done. To solve this issue, constituting FAC is very crucial, but setting up guidelines for the FAC is more important than its existence. On the contrary, before the beginning of the tenure, all the student government officials should be mandatorily asked to attend the fiscal disciplining workshop as part of the leadership training program.

A Bold Step Towards e-Governance has been already taken by SECC but should be taken by the IITM Student Government in totality. A well-dedicated page similar to that of IIT Delhi should be curated by the SLC Speaker so that all the achievements of the EC members along with those of the MITACS should be posted on the website regularly. The aim of the page should not only be to bring the IITM student government near to the GSB but to even bring it closer to the people outside IITM. Moreover, whenever the SLC Speaker has to conduct a referendum or a plebiscite then she should use this website to get the response of the GSB. As an alternative, the SLC Speaker can create a separate mobile app for student government officials to send notifications and updates to the GSB as and when required. This same referendum and plebiscite can be launched on the app so that students can participate in the IITM student politics seamlessly.

Abiding by the Rule of Law, to be more precise Students' Constitution should not only be the responsibility of the GSB but should also be the duty of the IITM administration including the faculty. There have been instances when the administration chose to bypass the Students' Constitution to enforce their decision by coercion instead of abiding by the Constitution. Such careless acts of the administration not only set bad precedence for the students to ignore the Students' Constitution but even abuse it for one's selfish gains. SECC being the custodian of the Students'

Constitution should take responsibility for safeguarding the Constitution at all costs by at least bringing it under the humble notice of the perpetrator.

Representation to the Online Degree Students needs a timely intervention in the IITM student government structure to provide equal opportunity to the students who are part of the IITM family uniquely. Treating online degree students as the 'other' is not helpful for anyone and is regressing the potential of the efficient governance that one can achieve by accommodating the ever-increasing number of online degree students. In my opinion, they are a more diverse set of students who can not only bring valuable insights to the table but can even help the existing student government to make IITM a better place. However, as per the Students' Constitution, those who pay Gymkhana fees are treated to be the GSB. Now do the online degree students pay the Gymkhana fees or not is not clear to me. But if they do then they should be made part of the IITM student politics at the earliest so that they can voice their concerns to the appropriate authorities.

The aforementioned suggestions are not set in stone but are the beginning of an unending endeavor where the welfare of the community is the greatest objective to be achieved. I agree that there are numerous issues I have not elaborated on in this book, as I believe there are already scholars who have published detailed works on these topics. One such issue is caste which I believe from my point of view to date has not maligned the student politics of IIT Madras because of the indomitable structure of the student government that was envisioned by the fathers of the Students' Constitution. There have been multiple attempts to highlight the caste distinctions within the IITs in different capacities but specifically emphasising the relationship between caste and student politics at IITs, at least at IITM is not known to me so far.

The day I entered IIT Madras, my parents told me that I was allowed to do everything that I wanted to do in my college life except to participate in the student politics of IIT Madras. I chose to not actively participate in the IITM student politics and so I ended up being the SECC & SEC Chief Commissioner. My father being a civil engineer graduate from NIT Silchar and an M.Tech graduate from IIT Delhi, had a very frightening impression of student politics which he didn't want me to experience during my college life. So I had the fortune of experiencing student politics in a very unique fashion by being part of the student bureaucratic organisation.

But I do not want the future students of IITM or in that case, students of any college to be cautioned by their parents because of the social evils that exist in the IITM or their dream college's student politics. I want future college students to live in a campus that nourishes their body and mind, to breathe in a campus that opens gateways to endless wisdom, to survive in a campus where co-existence is the rule of life, and to resonate themselves with a campus where the welfare of the community is the priority of every individual. This is because these same students will become the future responsible citizens of the world who will be making this world a better place to live in.

Hope to see you too as an active participant in student politics not because you got motivated by a book but because you discovered the true meaning of being a student.

References

(i) Indian Institute of Technology, Madras. (2017). *Students' Constitution of IIT Madras.* Retrieved December 21, 2024, from https://web.iitm.ac.in/secc/assets/pdf/Students_Constitution.pdf

(ii) Indian Institute of Technology, Madras. (2020). SECC *rules of procedure.* Retrieved December 21, 2024, from https://web.iitm.ac.in/secc/assets/pdf/SECC%20Updated%20Rules%20of%20Procedure.pdf

(iii) SECC. (2021, September 16). CEC *Shri Sushil Chandra at IIT Madras || Election Commission of India: Conducting elections* [Live stream]. YouTube. https://www.youtube.com/live/1aCfQwzvblc?si=8Q6ywdZWBfaJIHkk

(iv) SECC. (2024, January). *Election manual – Students' general elections 2024.* https://web.iitm.ac.in/secc/assets/pdf/Election_Manual_final.pdf

(v) Chanthrakumar, R. (2022, April 10). *IIT MADRAS College Elections! The untold side of IITs!* [Video]. YouTube.

https://youtu.be/SlNuWnx9GcQ?si=cq3uFX11EXKdxmml

(vi) Centre for Innovation, IIT Madras. (2023). *Built India's first blockchain-based voting portal system.* Centre for Innovation, IIT Madras. Retrieved January 5, 2025, from https://cfi.iitm.ac.in/achievements

(vii) Office of the Dean (Students). (n.d.). *Important apps & mass communication.* Indian Institute of Technology, Madras. Retrieved January 6, 2025, from https://dost.iitm.ac.in/iitmdost/important-apps--mass-communication

(viii) SECC. (2023). *Student Ethics & Constitution Commission.* Indian Institute of Technology, Madras. Retrieved January 7, 2025, from https://web.iitm.ac.in/secc/

(ix) Student Ethics & Constitution Commission. (2024). *Rules of procedure of SECC.* Indian Institute of Technology, Madras. Retrieved January 7, 2025, from https://web.iitm.ac.in/secc/assets/pdf/SECC%20Updated%20Rules%20of%20Procedure.pdf

(x) Office of the Principal Scientific Secretary. (2021). *Election Commission of India working with IIT Madras and CDAC for a more efficient voting system.* Government of India. Retrieved January 7, 2025, from https://psa.gov.in/CMS/web/sites/default/files/

psa_custom_files/Election%20Commission%20of%20India-IIT%20Madras.pdf

(xi) Gohain, M. P. (2024, April 29). *IIT-M charts a new course, uses blockchain for student body polls.* The Times of India. Retrieved January 7, 2025, from https://timesofindia.indiatimes.com/city/chennai/iit-m-charts-new-course-uses-blockchain-for-student-body-polls/articleshow/109671866.cms?pcode=461

(xii) Student Election Commission, IIT Madras. (2024, February 28). *#OPERATION100 | Theme launch | V. Palani Kumar | TNSEC | Voices of the state* [Video]. YouTube. Retrieved January 7, 2025, from https://www.youtube.com/live/q3ukmTpTdeI?si=h9aldBrHRL3eAWRB

(xiii) The Fifth Estate, IIT Madras. (2024, March 18). *All about elections | Sushant Jaswal Part - 2* (Insti FunDays) [Audio podcast episode]. Spotify. Retrieved January 7, 2025, from https://open.spotify.com/episode/7fqy2pAG8L2qEyJyymvIuX?si=o5J4DajfTSiS_dzv6X_1Tg

(xiv) IITM TV. (2024, April 29). *IIT Madras' blockchain election | SGE 2024: A documentary shortfilm* [Video]. YouTube. Retrieved January 7, 2025, from https://youtu.be/zv_y1odXuYM?si=P1npMjQPdKfmfE_5

(xv) Deka, M. (2024, November 12). *Life in an IIT: From rural roots to rocket science, this IIT Madras PhD student shares her journey. The Indian Express.* Retrieved January 7, 2025, from https://indianexpress.com/article/education/life-in-an-iit-madras-phd-student-shares-journey-from-rural-roots-to-rocket-science-jee-main-jee-advanced-9605228/

(xvi) Student Affairs Council, Indian Institute of Technology Delhi. (2022). *Student Affairs Council, IIT Delhi*. Retrieved January 7, 2025, from https://sac.iitd.ac.in/

(xvii) Harvard Extension School. (2015). *Student policies and conduct*. Retrieved January 7, 2025, from https://extension.harvard.edu/registration-admissions/for-students/student-policies-conduct/

(xviii) University Grants Commission. (2006). *Recommendations of the Lyngdoh Committee report.* Ministry of Human Resource Development. Retrieved January 7, 2025, from https://www.ugc.gov.in/oldpdf/students_pdf/lyngdoh_committeemhrd2712.pdf

www.ingramcontent.com/pod-product-compliance
Lightning Source LLC
Chambersburg PA
CBHW050019170726
48282CB00025B/471
* 9 7 8 9 3 6 7 8 3 0 1 3 0 *